M000020957

GIRLFRIENDS
DON'T
MATTER

HUMANITY DIVERSITY LLC
WAYNE PERRYMAN
PO BOX 256
MERCER ISLAND, WA 98040

GIRLFRIENDS DON'T MATTER

WHAT EVERY WOMAN SHOULD KNOW
ABOUT DATING, MEN, AND RELATIONSHIPS

CHERYL HASKINS

WinePressPublishing
Great Books, Defined.

WinePress Publishing (PO Box 428, Enumclaw, WA 98022) functions only as book publisher. As such, the ultimate design, content, editorial accuracy, and views expressed or implied in this work are those of the author.

Unless otherwise noted, all Scriptures are taken from the *New King James Version*. Copyright © 1982 by Thomas Nelson, Inc. Used by permission. All rights reserved.

Scripture references marked KJV are taken from the *King James Version* of the Bible.

Scripture references marked MSG are taken from *The Message*. Copyright © 1993, 1994, 1995, 1996, 2000, 2001, 2002. Used by permission of NavPress Publishing Group.

Scripture references marked NLT are taken from the *Holy Bible, New Living Translation*, copyright © 1996, 2004, 2007 by Tyndale House Foundation. Used by permission of Tyndale House Publishers, Inc., Carol Stream, Illinois 60188. All rights reserved.

ISBN 13: 978-1-60615-224-9
ISBN 10: 1-60615-224-6
Library of Congress Catalog Card Number: 2012903922

DEDICATION

To my husband, Pastor Aaron Lee Haskins Senior (January 6, 1960–October 25, 2009): I will be forever grateful for the impact this man had on my life for thirty-one years. He was a wonderful husband, father, grandfather, encourager, and friend. He loved me unconditionally, and in spite of myself, he "got" me. He always told me that if I wanted to help people, I could through my writing, encouraging others, speaking, and just being a friend. He was a true lover of people, an anointed saxophone player, worship leader, pastor, and friend to many. It brings me great joy every time I encounter people who tell me a story of how he impacted their lives. Through many people, his legacy lives on. I believe that he looks down from heaven and sees me doing what he encouraged me to do. Thank you, Honey!

To my son, Aaron Lee Haskins Junior (February 12, 1981–February 12, 2011): My dear son died at the young age of twenty-nine, but he left behind a legacy of "the turnaround."

He was a wonderful support to me after the death of my husband. He was a classic middle child—a peacemaker and a mediator, a true lover of people, just like his father. I will always be thankful that I was able to spend so much time with my older son. He stepped up to the plate and became my encourager, my helper, a companion, and a dear friend. He would stop by my house and say to me, "Hey, Mom, do you need anything?" I will always love and miss him. He encouraged me to write this book, *Girlfriends Don't Matter*. Like his Dad, he's looking down from heaven and can see that I've done that very thing.

To my father, CSGM Claude Andrew Dixon II (February 11, 1920–January 21, 2009): I credit my dad for giving me my sense of humor; even if it's a bit quirky; my determination to succeed; my enjoyment of talking a lot, and my belief in myself. He told me I was an idealist; yet at the same time, he understood that I was practical, spiritual, and realistic. I could talk to my dad about anything, and we would have lengthy conversations that would put the rest of the family to sleep. I miss my dad. I believe that my dad is standing with my husband and older son, reassuring them by saying, "That's my number-two daughter, Cheryl. She will make it; just watch."

To my other children, Latasha and Andrew: they have encouraged me, supported me, helped me navigate, and believed I could write a book. They were both so willing to have those "take over the world" conversations. I love them dearly and am so proud of how they have walked through the valley with me these last three years. They are still faith-filled, determined to make a difference, and upbeat about life.

Without Him (Jesus), I can do nothing, and I certainly could not have completed this book. Thank You, Jesus, for being there all the time, through all of my highs and all of my lows, my heartbreak, and my continued healing. Thank You for Your unfailing love, guidance, and amazing grace. I trust you, Lord!

CONTENTS

ACKNOWLEDGMENTS

I acknowledge my mom—Juanita Dixon—family, and friends who encouraged and supported me with their words and prayers through the process of my becoming an author.

I thank my staff, who walked this journey with me (they had no choice) and were supportive through this very challenging undertaking. I hope they are all inspired to go after their dreams too!

Thank you to my pastors: Gini, Judah, and Chelsea Smith, whose love, friendship, and support over the last nineteen years, especially the last three as we have grieved together, means everything as we all move towards a "new normal."

Thank you to the ladies who participated in my Straight Talk for Single Women's group. (I won't name anyone for fear of leaving some out.) They helped me to clarify a lot of the ideas by asking me to continually explain what I was trying to teach them. For the record, four weddings and a lot of much happier women have emerged from that group. Women can date, have fun, and enjoy the company of men. Who knows what good things are on the horizon?

Thank you to the professionals who helped to move my vision from my mind to paper, web, and picture form: Brandon Ellis, cover design; Michael Corley, illustrations; Laura Hunter, photography; and Stephanie Raines, whose editing made my book that much better. Thank you to Pastor Barbara Wright for her encouraging words after reading my first draft.

Finally, thank you to New York Times bestselling author Dr. Leslie Parrott for believing in me and writing the forward for my very first book. I am blessed.

FOREWORD

If you are a single woman over thirty who longs to be loved, every paragraph of this book has been written for you! From the first word to the last, Cheryl Haskins takes you on a heartfelt journey designed to prepare you to receive the desires of your heart. But be ready to be taken seriously! Cheryl will disarm every misconception you may be holding on to that prevents you from achieving committed love, starting directly with her title assumption that "girlfriends don't matter." She's practical, relevant, and grounded.

I've known Cheryl for more than a decade. She's the real deal. Everyone who knows Cheryl knows how much she relies on God. My husband, Les, and I have been deeply blessed by her shared ministry with her late husband, Aaron. Cheryl's candor, the warmth of her humor, and her razor-sharp insights combine to make her an excellent guide for any woman ready to take seriously her pursuit of marriage.

—Leslie Parrott
www.LesandLeslie.com
Author of *Real Relationships*

INTRODUCTION

I have written this book because I believe our thinking has shifted in the wrong direction in regards to dating, relationships, and marriage. If we don't start with our thinking, we are doomed to continue to make the same mistakes over and over again. I want you, the reader, to get to know me before diving into the chapters of this book.

I was widowed at forty-nine years of age. I became sensitized in a new way to the plight of single women above the age of thirty. I was married for twenty-nine years and never experienced the dating relationships women and men are subjected to today. I said "subjected to" on purpose.

There is a lack of respect in how relationships are approached, by both men and women. Poor treatment results in poor relationships.

There is a lack of respect in how relationships are approached, by both men and women. Poor treatment results in poor relationships. I was told by a very wise person that "how you start a relationship is the way you must maintain it." I have found this to be true in every arena of my life.

Things have changed in the past thirty years—for the worse, in my opinion. Seeing so many Christian and non-Christian women sad, depressed, desperate, jaded, negative, and generally unhappy over their single state motivated me to do something about it. Therefore, I started a small group at my church called Real Talk for Single Women and developed seven sessions to help women work through issues around wrong ideas and weird ways of thinking about themselves, men, and relationships. The weed-out session is entitled "Girlfriends Don't Matter." I would lose a few ladies the first week because they simply would not accept the statement as true. This book is an expansion on that one session because, inevitably, I would have one-on-one conversations to further explain what I meant.

> For thus says the LORD to the men of Judah and Jerusalem: "Break up your fallow ground, And do not sow among thorns."
>
> —Jeremiah 4:3

The above scripture could illustrate the idea that our minds are the ground in which seeds can germinate and grow, but now the ground is fallow and hard and covered in thorns. Fallow ground isn't bad ground; it was once ready for planting. It wasn't used for what it was intended and is now hard. The thoughts in this book will break up the ground in your mind and then fertilize, cultivate, moisten, and get it ready for a good seed (relationship) to be planted.

When I taught high school in Seattle (2001–2004), I would have the students memorize the following words and then recite them at the beginning of each day:

What I think about, I bring about.
So I choose to think good things about myself, my life, and my future.
I set goals and take positive steps to achieve them.
Yes!

I challenged my students in three areas: attitudes, thoughts, and actions. We talked a lot about their thinking: how it influenced their attitudes and eventually their actions. There are always reasons and circumstances we can use as excuses to justify wrong thoughts, attitudes, and actions, but I challenged them as I am challenging you. Think differently about life, and watch what new options unfold in front of you. You will begin to see things you never knew were there. I believe I have something to share that will help you; therefore, I am taking a risk and putting something out there for you and the rest of the world to consider.

I dated a couple of years as a young woman; married a great guy, who wasn't perfect; and stayed married to him "until death do you part," including during all the ups and downs that marriage can bring. My husband and I raised a family and worked together to grow together. I believe that what it takes to "get 'em," it takes to "keep 'em." I kept a great man, and I had parents who taught me how to be a woman and what to expect from men. I feel blessed my parents prepared me.

Consider this book a "girl talk," heart-to-heart, with no fluff or sugary coating—period.

SECTION ONE

SHAKE UP YOUR THINKING

For as he thinks in his heart, so is he ...
—Proverbs 23:7

The first four chapters of *Girlfriends Don't Matter* are intended to shake up and challenge your thinking. You will be challenged on three key concepts: being a girlfriend, the list, and the definition of dating. This is the foundation for you to progress in helping me to start a Relationship Revolution™. Chapter one will give you the background and a framework and a basis for where I am coming from in writing this book. I am confident that you will be changed and grow from the experience. Take the time to invest in yourself and consider the questions at the end of each chapter. Think about it.

Sow for yourselves righteousness;
Reap in mercy;
Break up your fallow ground,
For it is time to seek the LORD,
Till He comes and rains righteousness on you.
—Hosea 10:12

1

GET READY!

So get ready! I will state things as clearly as I possibly can. Time is up for cloaking the truth and being shielded from reality. You would know if I were playing games with you anyway, right? I am in a season, right along with you, of taking an assessment of where I am now and where I would like to be in the future. My life has completely changed, so it is time to take a look and evaluate. Please join me on this journey of self-rediscovery and reinvention. Don't let fear grip your heart or keep you from moving forward. Let go of thoughts like, *It won't work!* and, *I am never going to find anyone.* The right man will find you, Lord willing, as we get moving on this journey.

I love this statement: "No matter how long you stand in a garage, you will not become a car." I interpret that statement this way: if we want something new out of life, we must reposition ourselves mentally, emotionally, and physically to receive the new thing and be willing to let go of our old ways.

I am letting you know now that this book will contain quotes from the Bible. This is because the Bible is where all of my help and strength comes from. Jesus has proven His love for me over and over in my life, no matter what has happened—as if Jesus dying for the whole world were not enough. I have had some amazingly fun and happy times and some devastatingly sad, traumatizing times, but because of Jesus, I am still here. I want to live and continue to make a difference in the lives of people. I am inseparable from my faith in Jesus, and I know you will be encouraged, built up, and ready to embrace life in a new way after reading this book.

Aaron, my late husband, always used to tell me I could help a lot of people if I wanted to do so. He said that because I had a lot of natural common sense and wisdom, had the ability to find solutions, and could explain things and make them clear to others (how I miss his encouraging words). It was one of the qualities he appreciated about me, even when the truth was a little painful to hear.

Writing a book is no easy undertaking, and this is one of the most challenging learning experiences I have had so far in my life. Being a parent was tough at times because as I was raising children, I was also finishing college and being a wife. Then in the course of three years, I walked through the deaths of my father, husband, pastor, and older son. These occurrences changed me forever. I want you the reader to know that I simply refuse to give up, give in, or quit on life or myself. My faith keeps me strong and in my right mind, so I write from that perspective.

My faith keeps me strong and in my right mind, so I write from that perspective.

Who Is This Book For?

This book is for women in their mid-thirties and up who are single and want to be married. Women of a younger age, and men, can also benefit from the contents of this book. I am writing from an American cultural perspective. I realize there are cultural differences in how the courtship and marriage process takes place. However, what is most important is the spiritual perspective I bring. We are more than just our bodies and minds as women. Each of us is all woman: spirit, soul, and body!

I am jumping into the fray and going "counter culture," against conventional norms, in my approach. I want to cover what it means to be a woman of value, significance, and worth in today's world. After all of the progress we have made as women, we are less content with our lives than we ever have been. There was never anything wrong with wanting to be a wife and mother or work in the marketplace or do both.

Have you ever read Proverbs 31 in the Bible? The woman whose price is far above rubies is pretty amazing, whether she did all those things at once or one at a time. She took care of her man, her children, and her home; she ran a business and was respected in her community; and she reached out to those in need. It makes me sad to see so many women I know lacking in the area of relationships their lives. They are so accomplished in other areas of their lives (men are like this too, by the way). As a result, I have set out on a mission to make my contribution and do something about it.

Now, I don't want you to get worked up and angry while you are reading this book because I am not calling men out and talking bad about them. That is not the purpose of this book. Its purpose is to help you understand things from a man's perspective or, at the very least, from a different perspective. I also want women to regain their sense of value and worth. It may seem like you will never get a date or a man after doing the things in this book, but the opposite is true. I believe that if women "get it right," men will marry them. "It" refers to women's attitudes, thoughts, and actions.

Let me put it another way. What you are doing now isn't working, so why not become the woman you have always wanted to be? You may have thought you had to compromise to get a man. It is human nature for us to do as little as possible to get what we want. The last time I checked, men are humans too, and if you want to give it to them, they will gladly receive whatever you freely give (and not just sex).

What you are doing now isn't working, so why not become the woman you have always wanted to be?

Many times as associate pastors at our church, my husband and I would sit down with couples and try to help them with counsel from the Bible, prayer, and practical suggestions (that is where I would come in). I often described my husband's gift with people as "divine anesthesia," and my gift was the scalpel that cut out the "stuff." Aaron (my husband) died suddenly in October of 2009, so there is no more anesthesia. I promise to use a sharp scalpel, so there will be a clean cut that won't leave a scar. Better yet, let your desire to see the truth and a desire for real change become the anesthesia you need.

Right here in the beginning, I want you to hear my heart, catch the spirit of what I am saying, and be open to learning something new about yourself. There is so much hurt and pain in the world as a result of relationships. It is a proven fact that it is very difficult to erase bad experiences. In fact, it takes ten compliments to overcome one negative statement that is made. For some women who have had a lifetime, or a childhood, filled with negative words, this book will not be enough to overcome all of that. I hope it will at least lead you to start thinking differently and looking to the same source I look to for my identity and self-esteem—Jesus.

Three Tips to Start

To get you started on a new path, here are three tips I give the women who attend my workshops or single women's group.

Smile

A simple smile goes a long way in life. It should be a reflection that you are happy with yourself and with life in general. Smile at men. Give no angry glares or mean mugging. Stop looking over their heads or at the pavement, and no more hiding behind your severe, business-like glasses and walking like you are on a mission. All of that is a way to reject men before they can reject you. I cannot recall a time when I have smiled at someone when I was out and about and that person didn't smile back or say, "Hello." My sister gave me a CD last year entitled *Smile*, and the lyrics to that song are worth listening to. When you smile, you exude confidence; it says you are happy and approachable.

Make Eye Contact

Everyone wants to be seen and acknowledged. Validate people by looking at them. Just because you look at a man doesn't mean you are going to date him or marry him, but everyone likes to be acknowledged. Your confident smile and eye contact with a man today may benefit another woman tomorrow. He may get the nerve to approach someone he likes because a complete stranger was nice to him.

My daughter was in my first single women's group. She experienced firsthand what I just described. Her experience occurred in June of 2010, when she was dating several different men. She was practicing what you have been reading here. She was in line at a restaurant near her job, and she acknowledged each person in line with a smile.

Everyone wants to be seen and acknowledged. Validate people by looking at them.

After she purchased her lunch and sat down at a table, a handsome man approached her, one of the people she had smiled at. He asked if he could join her at the table. Of course, she said, "Sure." He proceeded to make small talk and finally just came out and thanked her for being nice and smiling at him. He told her his experiences with some ethnicities of women had not been positive and that he had shied away from approaching them as a result. He said her smile was a breath of fresh air and that he couldn't wait to tell his mother and grandmother about his experience. He asked her for her phone number, even though he had a girlfriend (hence the title of my book). My daughter went out with him once or twice, but she ended up meeting her husband a few months later and celebrated her first wedding anniversary on March 4, 2012.

Be Nice

A particular man may not be "the one," but he may know "the one." You do not have to leave a bad taste in anyone's mouth after they meet and talk with you. Many take dating in our present day too seriously. The thought that a man might

A particular man may not be "the one," but he may know "the one."

speak to you and hold a conversation when he is out with someone else is "abhorrent" and "reprehensible" to today's "daters."

There is no reason not to speak to someone or to be rude because a man has a girlfriend. I am not saying for you to flirt, display yourself, and fall all over someone's date. You can conduct yourself with some ladylikeness and common sense. You never know, the next time you see him, he may not have a girlfriend. If you were rude and nasty, you may have missed an opportunity!

I have a friend who shares her true story about this very situation. She attended my first group in the summer of 2010, along with my daughter, and was married just last September, 2011. Here is her story:

In the summer of 2010, Cheryl Haskins asked me to come up alongside and support her with a small group she was hosting in her home for single women. My first thought was that I didn't need to attend a small group discussion around dating. I was single at forty-three years of age and had never been married. However, as the singles group leader at a local church we both attended, I thought it would be good for me to attend this group to check out new content that I could possibly bring back to the single adults.

From the first five minutes of the first meeting, I found myself challenged and having to think outside the box regarding what I was being confronted with. I was intrigued, and it felt right; therefore, I committed myself not only as a support for Cheryl but also as a student. I opened up my head and my heart and threw away my judgments. One of

the most controversial statements I took away from
Cheryl's teaching was that
"girlfriends don't matter."
In other words, a girlfriend
is not a wife and so has not
sealed the deal on that man.
Once I understood the
meaning of that statement, I
was able to apply it.

In other words, a girlfriend is not a wife and so has not sealed the deal on that man.

Later that summer, I found
myself in Spokane, WA, for a reunion with family. On
Sunday, we visited a small Baptist church of maybe fifty
people. Sitting in the last row was a former boyfriend I had
dated seventeen years prior in San Jose, CA. He asked if I
was married. I replied, "No and you?"

He said, "No, but I have a girlfriend in Portland, OR."

My first thought was, *well girlfriends don't matter.* That statement freed me to feel comfortable to talk with him; whereas
before, I would have ended the conversation with, "Hello
and God bless you."

He encouraged me to get onto social media since I was
serving in a singles ministry. Monday morning, I created
an account on a social networking site and continued a
friendly conversation with my old, dear friend. I was able
to recognize that there was no chemistry between us any
longer, just a warm past.

A few weeks later, in September of 2010, and through
social media, I was able to reconnect with a man I dated
and became engaged to fifteen years ago. We eventually
went our separate ways without any closure. So now, fifteen

years later, we again found each other, reminisced, and reacquainted ourselves. It became known that he was pursuing someone else, and the statement again, "girlfriends don't matter," came to mind, and well, the rest is history. It again allowed me to be free to open up and talk with him. The girlfriend was not his wife but a girl he was pursuing to date. As we talked, there was forgiveness and restoration in our conversation. Only about a month later, he realized the woman he was pursuing wasn't the one for him.

We continued talking over the phone long distance since I was in Seattle, WA, and he was in San Jose, CA. We officially started our long distance dating about three months later. We got engaged and married exactly one year later, in September of 2011. I am married to the man of my dreams. It was meant to be, a God thing, ordained from the foundations of the earth, or however you want to look at it.

"Girlfriends don't matter" is not a principal to cause irresponsible destruction or disrespect to an existing, healthy relationship; however, it is the vehicle to use to examine one's life-long commitment.

—Liaza Nunn Richardson

Isn't that a great story? Are you ready to continue? I am. I believe in you and know a genuine desire for the truth is what you need to know God, to know yourself, and to enjoy life. Together let's start a revolution, a revival, and spark a fire in male/female relationships. Let's turn those marriage statistics around! More importantly, I want you to be empowered, encouraged, and equipped to lead a healthy, vibrant life in your relationships with men and to be found by that special someone. Happy reading—get ready for change—if you want it!

The Girlfriends Don't Matter Dictionary

It is important to define some terms to help you better understand my meaning as you read through the book. So read this first. Do not pass go. Do not collect $200 dollars.

Commitment: Simply put, commitment to men is marriage, and nothing short of it. Now, as women, we define commitment rather easily. A man asks us out to coffee, sits next to us in church, or asks us to go with him to dinner on Valentine's Day! We read way too much into behaviors that are just the natural part of the getting-to-know-you process. Take a step back and breathe, and let the friendship unfold naturally. Now I am preaching to myself too. I am the first one to get impatient once I know what I want, but in this new season, I am learning that great things come to those who wait.

Courtship or Courting: this is the transition between friendship and engagement/marriage for couples. This is the time to go deeper in the relationship, become an exclusive couple, and meet family. The interjection of the romantic component happens here, and the couple explores whether or not the relationship can move toward engagement and marriage. If they learned about each other as friends, this time period should be relatively short compared to the friendship and the eventual marriage. It is important to note that courtship can lead back to friendship, which is not a bad outcome. If upon a closer look you realize you are not right for each other, it's better to find that out before the engagement or marriage than after.

Twenty-first Century Dating ("hanging out"): This is a serial, monogamous relationship in which a man and woman focus on each other solely, forsaking all others, making decisions, and involving themselves in each other's lives and families like they are married. This is weird in my book and needs to cease and desist immediately, right now. Stop it! In some church groups, couples do this with a group as a precursor to pairing off by themselves.

Traditional Dating (what I recommend): This is the process of going out with multiple men during the same time period (to movies, dinners, concerts, bowling, sporting events, picnics, dances). These men are your friends. There is no romantic component to the relationships, such as kissing, fondling, make-out sessions, or sex. I didn't say there would be no attraction. But if you leave the romantic component out, you will be able to get to know the men better and not have issues dating several men at once. Be honest, and let the men know you date other men. Trust me; it will be OK. I wish we could go back to the days when men had to get on our social calendar to get a date. OK, that may be a little extreme. Men date several women at once all the time, and sometimes they tell you and sometimes they don't.

Endless Engagement: This is the status similar to what I call the "forever fiancée," or when a couple never gets married. They may not live together, or worse yet, perhaps they do, and the relationship just goes on and on and on. Stop it! Face the truth that more than likely, he doesn't want to marry you. Again, more than twelve–eighteen months in an exclusive relationship without a serious move towards marriage is a NO! This is way too long; it only takes about six months to plan a great wedding. I'm just saying.

> *If you are over thirty and are in a long engagement, then that man doesn't want to marry you. He is just hoping for "husband privileges" without being a husband.*

Forever Fiancée—This is when the relationship status has been an engagement for more than eighteen months. I do not understand being engaged for years and years and years. If you are over thirty and are in a long engagement, then that man doesn't want to marry you. He is just hoping for "husband privileges" without being a husband. There could be exceptions, there always are, but don't fall for this one. I don't care how nice the ring is either. If he finally ends the engagement—keep the ring; think of it as payment for time wasted and services rendered.

Friendship: It seems really strange to have to define this word, but the meaning has been lost in this new world of social media. Here is the dictionary definition:

- *A person attached to another by feelings of affection or personal regard*
- *A person who gives assistance*
- *A person who is on good terms with another*

Using this definition, you could be friends with more than one man at a time. You would be able to enjoy companionship without romantic entanglement. I don't mean that there may not be a physical attraction to some of your male friends. That doesn't mean you have to pursue it, or that you cannot go back to being friends if courtship doesn't lead to marriage. I know there are some people who say that men and women cannot be friends. If one of them is attracted to the other and it is not reciprocated, they have no choice but to be friends or acquaintances. They don't have to become enemies.

Girlfriend: This simply means you decided to be exclusive with one man and let him take you "off the market" because he might be "the one." You also believe he is as committed to you as you are to him, that this relationship is important and significant. As the title of this book indicates, I would disagree with you. I firmly believe a man shows his commitment by marriage. Even engagement is a *promise* to commit. I know men will give you push back on this, but let's see if they marry you.

"Beck and Call" Girl: This is when a man hints about his free time and expects you to drop what you are doing to be at his beck and call. For example, a man may say, "Hey, I am just hanging around getting things done at the house this evening."

Women with few principles respond with, "Oh, can I drop by and keep you company? I'll stop and pick up something for us to eat on my way."

A man truly interested in a relationship with you would say instead, "(Your name), I am free this evening and would like to know if you want to come over to my place for dinner?"

If you want to get married, you need to stop responding like a "beck and call girl." Some men are thrown off when you don't respond and think you aren't interested. No, your non-response just means you have standards.

When a man wants your company, he should ask you outright. This does require more from him. He has to pursue you and admit he wants to be with you. It is so sexy when a man steps up to the plate. We love it when a man is bold, don't we?

Husband Privileges: These are activities, time periods, and thoughts that should be reserved for the man who marries you. Everything in the chapters called "Desperate Wannabe Housewives" and "Escorts and Husband Privileges" spell out the meaning of husband privileges.

Instant Intimacy: This is the idea that a relationship is formed by the intensity of contact through frequency, over a short period of time, via electronic means and limited personal contact. For example, instant intimacy seeks to develop a relationship via e-mail and lengthy text messaging conversations. True intimacy begins and develops by actually speaking on the telephone or getting together in person. You can learn facts about someone from writing letters (e-mail), but a lot is missed in communication when you are not face-to-face.

If you are like me and quality time is one of your top two love languages, then you want a lot of face time because you desire 100% attention. Who knows what all a man could be doing while he is texting or e-mailing you? He could be working, talking on the phone to someone else, driving, or even grocery shopping. You cannot know for sure that you are the center of his attention.

Serial, Monogamous Relationship: This is a dating relationship with one man. You participate in these types of relationships one after another and watch year after year of your life go by and still no marriage. Sometimes these relationships evolve into endless engagements, children, and integration of finances. Serial monogamy is a big NO!

The List: The list is just that, it's a written and thought-through register of requirements and standards for the man you want to marry. There are a lot of good books out there about having your ten "must haves" and ten "can't stands." A list is only good if you have someone to apply it to. I was married for twenty-nine years, until my husband died. I had only three or four non-negotiables. In fact, I don't think it is possible to be happily married if your so-called "list" is too long. The main problem with "the list" is the fact that a list "to date" isn't the same as a list "to marry."

Questions to Consider:

1. Why did the author write this book?
2. What do you hope to gain or learn from reading it?
3. Are you ready to proceed, emotionally?
4. How are the three tips to get started working for *you*?

SO YOU WANT TO
BE A GIRLFRIEND?

OK, ladies, just admit it. You know it is true. Girlfriends don't matter to men as much as they do to us women. I am totally astounded by the concept of "in a relationship." What does that mean? You like somebody, he likes you. You may or may not be sleeping with him and sharing money, a house, and even children. I'm confused, and you should be too. Doing things that look like marriage won't make it marriage or a real commitment. Women reading this book want the real thing, right? I once tweeted the following: "It may look like a duck, walk like a duck, even quack like a duck, but it still isn't a duck." Meaning,

Girlfriends don't matter to men as much as they do to us women.

just because you do everything married people do, that doesn't mean you are married.

What does a social network status that says, "It's complicated," mean? Are you kidding me? Does that mean you are a wife and your man has a girlfriend; or are you the baby mama who is not the wife or the girlfriend? Or are you not sure what is going on? It amazes me that in the last twenty plus years, the status of dating has been elevated the same level as a real commitment, which is marriage. I know you don't want to hear that dating is not a real, committed relationship, but it's not! Dating is not the twenty-first-century version of marriage. Marriage is not outdated, or people wouldn't still be doing it every single day.

Please don't bring up the divorce rate, because you have to be married to get a divorce. If we quit pretending that dating, shacking up, and having kids with friends is an approximation of marriage, the divorce rate would go down considerably. I don't believe any of these non-marriage relationships necessarily prepare you for marriage, at least, not how you think it will. It is especially weird to see people put "in a relationship" on their status on social media sites, as if something has changed. I just want to say, "Duh Sherlock, if you aren't married, you are single." Just because you are a girlfriend, that doesn't mean you are not single. This may seem over simplistic, but this fact used to be common sense and common knowledge.

Brace Yourself

Where did the good ole days go? I guess when you are looking for anything but a real commitment, you create other labels in hopes you will get what you want from the other person (i.e., exclusivity, sex, money). Oh I know I am not being politically correct, but don't hold your breath while you wait for me to be, because I won't be. It might be a good idea to have a cup of coffee, a glass of wine, and a box of tissues handy while you are reading this.

Please don't get angry with me and start the attacks: *She doesn't know what she's talking about. My situation is different.* Your situation may be different, but there's a large majority of single women who are stuck, tired, and unhappy—women who want a real life with a man. Translation: these women want a marriage that is reasonably happy and lasting.

So, you want to be a girlfriend? If you are thirty plus, I ask you, "Why?" Aren't you done with that yet? Being a girlfriend is for teenagers and people in their twenties who are trying to figure out what they want, who they want, and what they are going to do when they grow up. I hope that by thirty years of age most of us know what we like and don't like. We don't need to be someone's girlfriend (an excuse to have sex in the relationship and make demands) in order to get to know the man as an adult, male friend and to determine if there is potential for something more.

I am a firm believer in that friendship leads to courtship that leads to marriage. That is if you want to be married. Personally, I cannot see myself being paraded around town at fifty plus years old and being introduced as someone's girlfriend. I know one popular book says if he doesn't proclaim by giving you a title, he is not serious. I agree. I'm just saying that "girlfriend" isn't the title a thirty plus-year-old woman should be aiming for.

If you are not his fiancée or wife, how a man handles himself when he is with you in public (his actions) can send a very strong message about how he feels about you. He may be trying to get his act together so he can propose to you, or ask to court you, because he knows you are "wife" not "girlfriend" material. Trust me, there is a distinction between the two. I say, let him work it out, and stay his fun, beautiful, dear friend!

Enjoy Yourself

Imagine it with me right now. You are out with a man you really like, and you are not his girlfriend because he knows how you feel about girlfriend status. He introduces you to his friends, "This is Elena, my dear friend!" as he puts his arm around your waist and gives his buddies a look that says, *Don't even think about it; she's mine. I'm working on stuff.*

You just smile sweetly and shake hands and say, "It's so nice to meet you." Keep in mind that unless you have agreed to date him exclusively, you can date other men too! I didn't say you should move in with, sleep with, have children with, and share money with him or with other men too! I said just date.

I am not advocating disrespecting other women who are "dating" a man or are considered girlfriends. I am trying to help you understand how far we have strayed in our culture from how to build genuine, long-lasting, loving, and committed relationships. This is about your attitude in life. Don't get a nasty attitude towards a man because he has a girlfriend and he dared to speak to you or smiled at you. The next time you see him, he may not have a girlfriend, and your bad attitude will have left a bad taste in his mouth for you.

I dislike the deception that says if you are dating someone you are not single. I hate to break the news to you, but if you are not married, you are single. I keep saying this because it is a needed mind-set change. A man who has a girlfriend is single, and so is she. They both should treat people well, because they may never move to courtship and marriage. Why burn every bridge along the way, thinking, *He is the one this time.*

I hate to break the news to you, but if you are not married, you are single.

A Simple Example

I promise I am not making this up, but my late husband, Aaron, had a girlfriend when I met him. I only saw her once and never did anything to move in on her. Aaron just kept talking to me, and I would say, "Hi," when I saw him, not avoid him like the plague, or be mean because he had a girlfriend. Next thing I know, he is asking me out, and I said, "Yes." From that point on, he gave me his four tickets for every Washington State University basketball home game (he was on the team). I never found out what happened to the girlfriend. She disappeared off the scene.

At the time, I was eighteen years old, and he was nineteen years old. We dated for a few months, and I told him, "I don't want to be your girlfriend. I want to be your wife and the mother of your children." Needless to say, I scared him to death, and I don't recommend being that direct. He didn't speak to me for almost a year afterward and quickly found a different girlfriend.

Guess what? I still had the four courtside tickets behind the bench to every game, because he wanted *me* to have them. I guess his girlfriend sat in the student section. I dated (not slept with) other guys and had fun freshman and sophomore years of college. I even told one of Aaron's girlfriends that he would marry me. Well, he did. I became his wife and the mother of his children. His girlfriends just never bothered me; he didn't belong to them or to me. I knew when he got serious, he would look my way; and when he did, I was smiling.

I knew when he got serious, he would look my way; and when he did, I was smiling.

Just Let Go

To get the most out of this book, you have to be willing to let go of the concept that being a man's girlfriend is significant, because it is not to men. I don't care what they tell you to get you to focus on them only. Do not let a man take you off the market or, better said, make you unavailable to date other men if he is not courting you.

The more I say this to women, the more I realize how very wacked-out and messy relationships between men and women have become. I haven't had one man yet pretend ignorance when I asked them to comment on the idea that girlfriends don't matter. The most frequent response I get is, "Well, they don't!" This doesn't mean they aren't into the women they are dating; the man might even really like her. However, the real deal is, to quote one man, "There are plenty more where that came from." This statement is so telling. It simply means there are a lot of women who are girlfriend material and very few they see as potential wives. I know this is tough to hear, but why be in denial? I am not telling you this to make you angry, but rather to make you savvy and confident.

Some men will get defensive and say their girlfriends are very important to them and that they are serious. The proof is in the pudding. If the man is seeing a confident woman who knows her value, it is a different story than if he's seeing a lonely woman who just wants to be in a relationship when Valentine's Day comes around. I would love to check with these men in a year and see if they are married or not. Some simply don't want to get married or, at least, not for the time being, so why have a girlfriend? To get the benefits of marriage, women are so willing to give without being married.

I was recently at a women's conference where one of the speakers said this: "You are a wife before you get married because the Bible says in Proverbs 3:23, 'A man who finds a wife finds a good thing and obtains favor from the Lord.'"

It is time to give up the idea that being a girlfriend is as significant as we want it to be. Are you ready to let go? You can do it, and you will be a better woman for it. You will get hurt far less in your relationships with men in the future.

Questions to Consider

1. Do you agree or disagree about what it means to be a girl-friend? Why or why not? List your three main objections or why you support the statement.
2. Have you seen a girlfriend who didn't matter in real life? Describe the situation.
3. Do you think it is important to continue to have the girl-friend experience after you are past twenty-five years old? Why or why not?

My grandson had his orientation day for sixth grade, and his mom was excitedly telling me about his ASB (Associated Student Body) card, changing classes, and how she couldn't believe that he was in sixth grade. She was crying like it was literally the first day of school ever. I could hear my grandson in the background saying, "Let me talk to my grandmother. Let me talk to my grandmother. I have to tell her something."

He got on the phone and told me that the eighth graders were showing them all around. After the big assembly, a cute eighth grade girl came and sat down next to him. She told him she wanted to be his girlfriend for the school year. (Wow, the boldness sure starts early.) My grandson said, "No way!"

She asked, "Why?"

He said, "Because girlfriends don't matter."

I asked him what she did, and he said, "She just marched off."

I didn't know this book would keep my handsome grandson safe on his first day of sixth grade, but you never know who is listening and what they will do with what you say.

THE LIST

Why do you need a list for what you want in a husband if you aren't even dating, especially if no one is asking you out or approaching you? It seems to me that the women with the longest lists are the ones who have been single the longest and aren't dating. This is counter-intuitive. If you are getting dates, your list should be shorter, not longer. Men and women get this one wrong. Is there a correlation between how long of a list you have and the number of dates you don't have? It is premature to have a list of demands for what you want in a husband, especially when you are not even dating or don't have any male friends to speak of.

What I mean by having male friends is that you have men you talk to, see, or go on outings with. These would be men in whom you are not romantically interested.

I am now working on this myself and developing some male friends. It is tough at first to communicate to a man that you want to be friends. It is nice to have much older, single, male friends in addition to male friends ten and fifteen years younger to gain different perspectives. It is also helpful to maintain relationships with married couples. They can be helpful in bouncing off ideas and questions, talking about things you did or said, and for getting wise counsel about dating.

The other challenge I have with comprehensive "husband lists" is that they make us feel obligated to draw them up in the name of having a standard. However, can we or do we even live up to them? I have seen lists that read like this:

The man I date must be:

- Good looking (hot).
- A homeowner.
- A strong man of God.
- A leader.
- In good shape.
- From a good family.
- Never before married/never divorced.
- A virgin (believe it or not).

The man I date must have:

- A good job.
- A nice car.
- A sense of humor.
- Potential to be a good father.
- A variety of interests.
- No children.

After reading many of these lists, my first question is, "Do you measure up to all of these traits yourself?" This is a fantasy man, the result of watching too much television and reading too many romance novels. I hear these things from women who only go to work and church, have no other interests, make very little effort on their own appearance, rarely smile or make eye contact with men, and have family issues of their own.

This is the point: the "to date" list is not the same as the "to marry" list. I know from experience that your "to marry" list better not be longer than five items or you will be very unhappily married. No one can live up to a long list of expectations.

This is the point: the "to date" list is not the same as the "to marry" list.

Some women say, "Why should I waste time with a man I wouldn't marry?" My first response is, of course, my classic, "Wow!" This question usually comes from a woman who can't even get a date, so how is it that she is wondering about wasting time? I don't think taking time to get to know another person and the two of you finding out more about each other is a waste of time. Basic, normal, human relationships are not a waste of time.

You may find you have hang-ups that are keeping the man you want away from you. You may find you aren't very good at conversing about a variety of topics and you have a tough time being face-to-face with a man you don't know well. You think that when it is the right man or the one God has for you, everything will just click. Let me tell you right now: if you are in your thirties or older and are still single, you have developed habits, thought patterns, and attitudes you are aware of and not aware of that may be a turn-off to the opposite sex.

I have to think about this myself since I am newly single. I have to make adjustments and understand that the open, wonderful, intimate communication I was used to with my late husband is a little overwhelming to these modern, single men.

I am amazed by how men just expect "a game" and dishonesty from women. My honest, direct approach is probably frightening for most men. Even the men who say they like it still try to play their regular game with me, a game that is challenging, fun, and frustrating all at the same time. My thoughts are, *Let's just get to the point; we are into each other! Let's just acknowledge it and leave out all of the games.* Oh I know it is simple, but far from easy, and probably wishful thinking on my part, but I am an idealist.

Now don't go off the deep end and think you aren't supposed to exercise good common sense. Remember, I am talking to women ages thirty and above who should know it isn't wise to date a dangerous person or someone who breaks the law.

No Pressure Dating

I have been asked, "What if the man who wants to date me is not on the same page with me spiritually?" I understand where this question is coming from, but can you just go back in time with me and remember junior high and high school? Did we ask this question? No, we did not, maybe because we knew we weren't going to run off and marry the boy.

Just think how relaxed you will be with a man who "isn't on the same page spiritually." You won't be thinking about wedding dresses while on your date just because he asked you to coffee. You can have a conversation and work on being exciting and interesting. You can discover what you bring to the table. This is a date with no pressure except to be you. You may have only this one date with this particular man. What a novel experience.

Women who haven't dated in years (due to a variety of circumstances and/or due to having an exhaustive list) need all the practice they can get. I encourage you to toss the list aside for ninety days to six months, use your common sense, and

I encourage you to toss the list aside for ninety days to six months, use your common sense, and get out there and have some fun.

get out there and have some fun. Talk to men, enjoy their company and conversation, and get to know them without kissing, heavy petting, and having sex.

Yes, I have to keep saying this because it seems to come with the territory these days. I am still stunned that women will have sex on the first date or even the tenth, and with man after man as they go from relationship to relationship. Call me old-fashioned if you want to, but it is what it is.

I have had men thank me for providing them an opportunity to interact with well-dressed, interesting, quality women of all shapes and sizes without the pressure of being on a date by today's standards. I know I am on the right track with this.

Don't get me wrong: if keeping your date list is working for you, by all means, work it. I am suggesting you don't need it to date by the old-school definition. After all, the man you go out with may not be "the one," but he may know "the one." He may remember you when he's thinking of one of his friends and then introduce you to that guy.

When a List Is Useful

There are practical, logical, and even spiritual reasons for developing a date list. Lists help to keep you focused on what you are looking for. Lists can also rule everyone out (at least all flawed humans on earth) and include some people who may be too perfect.

I was having a conversation with a particular man, and while he has a list of things he can't stand and things he must have in a woman, on his profile on a dating site, he indicates no real preferences and casts a broad net. His profile is basically saying, "I am open for business; everyone apply." While we women have all of these very specific criteria in the dating game, men don't. They don't apply the same standard to women they date as they do to the women they consider marrying. It's like the

We women, on the other hand, turn the funnel upside down and try to squeeze one man down (if he meets all the criteria on our list) and only one at a time.

funnel approach: get as much as you can in the top and squeeze out a few qualified candidates out of the bottom. We women, on the other hand, turn the funnel upside down and try to squeeze one man down (if he meets all the criteria on our list) and only one at a time.

I don't like either of these approaches. What happened to normal dating as friends: getting to know people, then acknowledging that one may start to stand out more than the others, and then making the move forward? This high-stakes, emotional dating that takes place now is tiring and wastes a lot of time. Ladies, we could get a real Relationship Revolution™ going if we dumped these lists for a while. The least that could happen is men and women would learn once again how to enjoy each other's company without being under the pressure to define the relationship beyond friendship.

Let's imagine a world without lists. Let us assume the basic requirements are in place: the person is not a serial killer, a lawbreaker, or an otherwise dangerous individual. This means after looking at profiles on a dating website, you select several different men to go out with. You go out to coffee, have a nice conversation, and during that conversation, you find out information that you like or don't like about that man. Let's say the next day you go out with another guy. You go to dinner, a movie, have a nice drive home, and learn that you actually have some things in common. Later in the week, you meet another man for coffee. You learn you actually go to the same church and you didn't even know it.

Based on these three interactions with three different men, you decide all of them are worth going out with on another date. After a second date with one of the gentlemen, you find he is not a good match for you. However, you have a friend who you think might like him, so you introduce the two of them.

One of the reasons I encourage you to go out on dates without these full-blown lists is because you need practice. Many women who are over thirty-five years old, haven't been on a date in so long that they have lost their ability to even communicate with men in a normal manner. Why is a list important when you need a lot of practice? As long as you exercise basic common sense and good judgment, you should feel free to meet men and get to know them without a list.

When you're comfortable dating, having conversations, and enjoying the company of men, then you can start using a list. Remember what I said earlier in this chapter, that a "to date" list is different from a "to marry" list. Just try not using a list, and see how it works for you. When you get a man who has asked you to be exclusive in dating him, you can find plenty of books and websites to help you with what should be on your list.

Finally, I am going to say this again: if no one is asking you out and you are not dating on a regular basis, you do not need a list. When you have men to choose from who you consider potential spouses, then you can develop a list, but remember to keep it short. I want you to get used to just being out there, enjoying your life, enjoying the company of men in an appropriate manner, and getting used to being in your own skin. When you're there, the rest will follow.

Questions to Consider

1. Why do I have a list?
2. What are five items on my "to date" list?
3. What qualities do I have to see on a profile to select a man to date?
4. Are you ready to take the "Ninety-Day Challenge" and just have some fun?

DEFINITION OF DATING

Dating used to be a simple, fun way to get to know the opposite sex. Typically, parents would let their pre-teen to mid-teenage daughter go out with a group of friends. Once the sweet sixteen birthday hit, the girl could go on her first real date with a boy. At least that is how it was for me. It was a rite of passage. Attending dances in junior high and high school, going to sporting events, and participating in after-school activities were all ways to socialize and learn about appropriate interaction with boys. In addition, if the young lady belonged to a church or a social activity group, she had plenty of opportunities to be involved, go places, and meet boys who didn't necessarily live in her neighborhood or go to her school.

This is the pattern I wanted to use with my own children, but it ended up being slightly modified due to the fact that my husband was raised in a far more religious environment than I was. We wanted relationships between the sexes to be normal for our children, not a weird, overly religious approach that makes relating to each other awkward. We offered opportunities for them to entertain their male and female friends. They were able to interact with their friends at home, on outings, while participating in sports, and when involved in other extracurricular activities. I had many conversations with our children about the boy/girl thing in a normal and fun way. Why not let your children learn in an environment where you are there to help them process and navigate? When they grow up, they will make their own decisions. If they make bad ones, it won't be due to ignorance.

I work with young people both in and out of the church, and it's shocking to me how they are practically afraid to interact with the opposite sex in a normal manner. It's funny, men and women who are in their late twenties and early thirties are no different than the young people. They are afraid to have normal friendships, one-on-one. Who made up the weird rule that if you talk to a girl, you want to marry her, or if a girl goes to have a soda with a guy, she wants to marry him? That is straight up weird and ridiculous. This is where I feel sorry for men. They can't even act naturally and approach a woman because they are attracted to her, nor can they ask her out to see if they will like more than her looks. They must endure all of her friends saying, "Oh my goodness, girl, is he the one? If he's not, you shouldn't go out with him."

Who made up the weird rule that if you talk to a girl, you want to marry her, or if a girl goes to have a soda with a guy, she wants to marry him?

It Isn't a Duck!

Where did these new norms come from? Below is an excerpt from a blog post I wrote that captures where I believe dating is today:

It is a very different world than thirty years ago when it comes to relationships between men and women. It saddens me to see how far things have drifted from what is healthy physically, emotionally, and spiritually. The casual approach to relationships and instant intimacy created by technology makes me laugh out loud at times. When I hear women say things like, "We've been texting for over a week, and I feel so close to him," I want to warn them that "seeing is believing," and sometimes even that ends up being a front.

I went on a date recently with a younger man. After a two hour, face-to-face conversation, he asked me over text, "Will you be my girlfriend?" You have got to be kidding me!

I am serious about starting a "Relationship Revolution™"! I want both women and men to clear their heads, take a breath, and start thinking. It appears we are caught up in a world of sound bites, reality TV that is only a reality for a select few, and living our lives by getting excitement vicariously through others. Things are simple when it comes to relationships, but by no means easy. I tweeted recently about relationships attempting to approximate or simulate marriage. "It may try to look like a duck, quack like a duck, and walk like a duck, but it still isn't a duck."

We have come a long way, baby, and we are going in the wrong direction. Don't get me wrong: I believe technology is great and has its place in our relationships. However, the speed at which we attempt to build relationships is counterproductive to the endgame of intimacy, which is being known and truly knowing someone else.  Getting to know someone as a friend is the purpose for dating. We need to break out of the mentality of dating to mate. The only reason we think dating is serious is because we are adopting a modern definition of the word.

We need to break out of the mentality of dating to mate.

In conversations with women and men, the phrase "hanging out" is used to describe spending time with each other or dating. We need to reclaim the definition. Here is dictionary definition of dating, found at www.thefreedictionary.com:

- An engagement to go out socially with another person, often out of romantic interest
- One's companion on such an outing

American society continues to adjust the norms of acceptable behavior between men and women. As a result, dating is considered a serious relationship. This is an extreme reaction to the problem with marriage in our society. It is human nature, especially for women, to want commitment and security; therefore, men are not proposing marriage. In reaction to this, women have elevated dating to a more serious place to satisfy their need for commitment. For men, this commitment need is not the same. They get away with less of a commitment because women are satisfied with supposed exclusivity with a man. This type of relationship now serves as a substitute for the real commitment that marriage is. So guess what a woman gets to be? A girlfriend. You know what I think about that when it comes to men: girlfriends don't matter.

Just Have Fun!

When we look back in history at past dating or mating trends, we see that it has never been easy to find that special someone. The biggest difference I see that has happened over time is that now we have couples who are in serial, monogamous relationships that they call dating. These relationships operate like marriages without the couple being married.

Why would anyone want to work that hard without a real commitment? I haven't any idea. What happened to the days of going out with men to get to know them as friends? What happened to discovering if you have anything in common? What about going out just to enjoy each other's company? If you are not married, you do not have the grace (blessing) to live with a person day in and day out. Nor do you have the proper perspective and attitude of forgiveness.

I was having a girl's day out with my mom. While we were getting pedicures, we were discussing what it would be like to start dating again. It was surreal for my mom and me to be widows and talking about dating. Neither of us saw widowhood coming. In the middle of our conversation, my cell phone started ringing. The call was from a male friend of mine. After I finished the conversation, my mom started telling me how I needed to just go out with him or someone else and have some fun. That is what dating is all about.

As I work with single women, I hear them say, "I am not going to settle." Women who want to marry and have a family must change their definition of dating; otherwise, they

Women who want to marry and have a family must change their definition of dating; otherwise, they will be settling.

will be settling. I hate to break the news to you, but you have already done it. When you decide that a serial, monogamous relationship outside of marriage is commitment, you are settling if you want to be married.

Another strange phenomenon that has occurred in this new era of dating in the twenty-first century is when a couple becomes exclusive and they consider themselves no longer single. If you are not married, you are single. When you give a man your exclusive commitment as if you are married, you are on very dangerous emotional ground. This is why when women and men break up, they experience deep emotional pain in what should have been just a friendship, not a pretend or practice marriage.

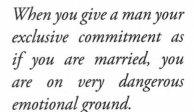

For the record, dating is not preparation or practice for marriage. Dating is building a friendship with someone of the opposite sex. Whether you move on to courtship with the person or not, if you build a genuine friendship, you will stay friends (more on this

When you give a man your exclusive commitment as if you are married, you are on very dangerous emotional ground.

in chapter nine). In fact, you should be dating or building friendships with multiple men at the same time. Yes, I said it; someone had to!

Redefining Dating and Marriage

If you decide that you are not going to date to build a friendship and you are simply going to jump from singleness to courtship and then to marriage, you will go through your dating phase after you are married. There is no substitute for getting to know someone. You can do it before you marry by becoming friends first, or you can do it after you marry, but you will do it.

I belonged to a ministry during my college years that brought couples together in one of the most unnatural ways I'd ever seen. Individuals would pray, then go to the pastor and submit a person's name, and if they matched up? A wedding! (I'm glad I was already married.)

Now, there is good fruit; most of the couples are still married today, over thirty years later, but many of those couples went through varying degrees of hell to become friends and fell in love after they were married. The success of their marriages was not due to the weird or more "spiritual" method that brought them together. Their success was due to the fact that their relationship with God was genuine and faith-filled, so they persevered.

Serial monogamy has no place in friendship dating. If you cling to the modern definition of dating, then I have just crushed your proverbial toes. So be it. Younger women especially are missing out on the opportunity to develop their social skills and confidence. I made it clear in the first chapter where I am coming from, and by no means am I suggesting any level of poor, unseemly behavior on the part of women or men. Let's get real. We have allowed celebrities and the media to redefine dating into something unrecognizable and stressful. The whole boy-meets-girl process, when attraction is present, brings a level of anxiety all on its own, without morphing the relationship into a pretend or practice marriage.

The last thing I want to say about redefining dating is that attraction to a man is not an indication that he is the one. If you think back over your life, since the time you were a pre-teen, there have been many boys and men you were attracted to over the years. This is a natural part of life. What you do with the attraction is what determines whether or not a romantic relationship will ensue. Attraction happens, but that is not the only determinant of whether or not the person is suitable for you as a husband.

Learn how to discern this now, because even after you are married, you could be attracted to a man who is not your husband, or at the very least, you could notice he is handsome or "hot." Visual attraction seems acceptable when speaking about leading men in movies, even if you are married; but no woman readily admits her visual attraction to the guy at work, or her realization that the guy next door is "hot," especially if a Christian woman is the one attracted. This is proof positive that appropriate management of attraction is a life-long skill.

Questions to Consider

1. What is the purpose of dating to you?
2. Do you agree or disagree that the definition of dating has changed? Why or why not?
3. Could you date more than one man at a time? Why or why not?
4. What are your biggest fears about dating?

I was talking to one of my son's friends about writing this book. The young man literally asked me twenty questions about the whole friendship-leads-to-courtship issue. He said, "Use me in your book; it's OK." He was intrigued by the idea of leaving the physical aspects out of the friendship and truly trying to get to know women as real friends. He admitted, "That would be a challenge since women give it up so easily."

I asked him if he was looking for a wife or just to have a good time, because there is a difference. He agreed with me that he was just out there having a good time.

This new definition of dating is throwing off the natural process of getting to know the opposite sex. My son's friend was thrilled with the idea of dating several different women at once. Well, of course he was, but I challenged him to do so with no sex, kissing, or heavy petting: just form friendships. You know what his next question was? "OK, Cheryl, how do I meet a nice, quality woman?"

SECTION TWO

RELATIONSHIP BOOT CAMP™

WARNING

The purpose of the next four chapters is to challenge the conventional norms of how women think and relate to men. You may get angry or sad. Be assured that your anger or sadness will only be temporary because I won't leave you there. Are you ready to break the cycle of moving from relationship to relationship that is leading nowhere and is a waste of your precious time?

This process is not for the faint-hearted. This will be more like real physical boot camp. It is for women who are ready to get results. Get tissues or a glass of wine if you need it, but take the plunge, and know you will be better for it. At the very least, you will have another perspective to consider.

This is the section of the book where I am saying a lot of things others think about but simply won't say. I am saying them because someone has to! Let's break down the thinking that is compromising your value as a woman in your own eyes as well as in the eyes of the men you deal with.

It is time to shake up your thinking about dating, men, and relationships.

Ready, set, go!

> [15] When the king smiles, there is life;
> his favor refreshes like a spring rain.
> [16] How much better to get wisdom than gold,
> and good judgment than silver!
> [17] The path of the virtuous leads away from evil;
> whoever follows that path is safe.
>
> —Proverbs 16:15–17 NLT

"I'M WAITING ON THE LORD" ·

(And other sayings you quote when you are older, desperate, and still single …)

Now this is a difficult chapter to write because we are about to touch a taboo subject or sacred cow, especially among church people. Even the subtitle of this chapter is meant to provoke. The more these statements are said, the longer it will take you to get married. I feel obligated to challenge that mentality for women (and men, for that matter).

In a traditional world, men typically do the asking, and women have to wait to be asked; therefore, if a man is not married, it's because he hasn't asked anyone to marry him. For men who say they want to be married but are not, I ask, "Who have you asked?" Reality TV shows exist where women are doing the asking, and I have heard stories from my friends about women who have done the asking, but I am an old-fashioned girl. I want men to step up, bring a nice ring (i.e., one where I can see the diamonds without a magnifying glass—a matter of investment and sacrifice), and say those wonderful words (or some variation of): "Will you marry me?"

Women are famous for making statements such as:

- "Good things come to those who wait."
- "I want to be pursued; that's what men are supposed to do."
- "God's timing is perfect."
- "I am waiting for God's perfect will, not His permissive will."
- "If he is for me, he will find me wherever I am."
- "If it's the Lord's will, then I will get married."
- "When I meet him, I will know."

Not Just for Christian Women

This chapter may seem like I'm writing primarily to Christian women or faith-based women; however, many women will say to you, "I'm waiting for the right man to come along," or, "I'll just know when he's the one; getting along won't be difficult, it won't be a struggle. I will know." The idea here is one of waiting and hoping to see if the right guy is just going to stumble across your path. This is the equivalent of waiting for the delivery man to drop off a package while you are actually at home, then your eyes meet, and wow, you realize the delivery guy is your Prince Charming! That is, of course, if he is not already married, which most seem to be. The same applies to paramedics, firefighters, police officers, and other potentially eligible men.

This is challenging because I can remember being asked the question many times, "How did you know Aaron was the one?" I usually respond and say, "I just knew." But here's my point: I wasn't waiting around for Aaron to happen upon my life. I was at college, living life, registering for classes, and getting ready for orientation week. There was a dance where lots of freshmen were going, and I went. I went to the dance to meet people, have a nice time, and find out what the college social scene was all about. Lo and behold, I met a lot of people, both men and women, and I met Aaron.

I know this may seem overly simplistic, but I put myself in a place to meet a man. We didn't get together right away, and I went to many other social events and met many different men. I knew a lot of boys from high school who went to my college as well. If we think back to our younger days and revisit them, we will find it really isn't that hard to meet people.

I'm Available

I can hear you saying it, and I know you're thinking it: "I don't want to go out to all those clubs and bars to meet a man."

I hear you. I don't either. This is where I think this new way of doing life and dating isn't all it is cracked up to be. We've lost the ability to just have social activities where men and women can interact in a non-threatening manner and just enjoy each other's company.

What happened to gatherings where you have dinner parties where couples or singles can come? What happened to belonging to organizations that put on events? What happened to your friends—married or single—introducing you to people? What happened to meeting people in coffee shops or on the commute to work on the bus or train? What happened

We've lost the ability to just have social activities where men and women can interact in a non-threatening manner and just enjoy each other's company.

to striking up conversations with total strangers? With all the technology and all the accessibility that we have today, we have lost the simple ability to make human connections.

As I was thinking about this chapter, an old song by Burt Bacharach came to mind called "Wishin and Hopin" ("Wishin and Hopin" by songwriters: Bacharach, Burt / David, Hal, recorded by Dusty Springfield). Here are the lyrics:

Wishin and hopin and thinkin and praying,
planning and dreaming each night of his charms,
that won't get you into his arms.

So if you are looking to find love you can share,
all you gotta do is hold him and kiss him and love him
and show him that you care

Show him you care just for him, do the things he likes to do,
wear your hair just for him,
cause you won't get him thinkin and a prayin, wishin and a
hopin

Wishin and hopin and thinkin and praying,
planning and dreaming his kisses will start,
that won't get you into his heart

So if you're thinking of how great true love is,
all you gotta do is hold him, and kiss him and squeeze him
and love him,
Yeah just do it and after you do you will be his

Show him you care just for him, do the things he likes to do,
wear your hair just for him,

cause you won't get him thinkin and a prayin,
wishin and a hopin

Cause wishin and hopin and thinkin and praying,
planning and dreaming his kisses will start,
that won't get you into his heart

So if you're thinking of how great true love is,
all you gotta do is hold him, and kiss him and squeeze him
and love him,
Yeah just do it and after you do
you will be his
you will be his,
you will be his!

The point in this song is not to sit around waiting for something to happen but to be actively waiting. I'm not advocating that you go to a man who you're attracted to and grab him and kiss him and squeeze him like the song might suggest. I am saying you need to make the effort to show that you are available, that you're willing to engage in getting to know someone. You can't do that sitting at home on your couch every night. You have to be willing to get out of your comfort zone, do something different, and even do something scary—like go out.

I remember the first New Year's Eve when I went out after my husband died. I went out with a couple of single girlfriends, and I've never done that before. I bought a new dress, and I styled my hair. I made every effort to look nice and have a good time. We went to a singles' event, and saying it was disappointing is an understatement. It's difficult for me to understand how far we have fallen from the ability just to have a good time. It seems tough to create a nice environment for people who aren't married in which they can socialize and get to know each other.

Show Yourself Friendly

Now, ladies, we could blame the men and say they should be the initiators, they don't know how to approach women, and so on. I agree with you. These things are true, but the society in which we live now has created a dynamic where natural, human interaction has become unnatural. In addition, it may be hard to believe that men get nervous about approaching women for fear of being rejected. Although they do, hence the words to the song I quoted, "You have to show them that you care," we just can't sit around, stand around, walk around, and just be out there and not convey in a positive, ladylike way that we are interested in being approached. We have to get out there, go to events, talk to men in public settings, be friendly, smile, and make eye contact with people. We shouldn't be lazy, sit around, do nothing, and hope some wonderful man will sweep us off our feet and marry us.

We shouldn't be lazy, sit around, do nothing, and hope some wonderful man will sweep us off our feet and marry us.

Proverbs 18:24 says, "A man who has friends must himself be friendly." Many of us want men to approach us. We want to be found, courted, and married, but we aren't friendly. Please don't get caught up in the mind-set that if you smile and are friendly, somehow you're being a flirt or a tease and stepping over the line. We have to get out of our comfort zones to some degree.

Being nice used to be natural for us when we were children. Yet some children were shy and a little more reluctant to make friends, but what did our parents say? Our parents told us, "Now Janie or Johnny, be nice. Talk to the kids at school so you can make friends." Somehow as adults we feel this is no longer necessary.

I recognize there are very valid reasons for looking before you leap and for not considering every man as a potential husband. There have been a lot of books written about waiting for the right man and not missing the will of God for your life. Many of these books advocate not dating at all and even going to the extreme of letting someone match you up with the right person. There is no fool-proof method out there to find, or be found by, a husband. If you do not lead a normal life—a life that requires interactions in many different settings with men—you will dramatically reduce your chances of getting married (unless *not* getting married is what you want).

During one of the sessions in my small group, we talk about the conversations we have about men and with the men in our lives. Sometimes we can self-sabotage by not dealing with past issues and hurts related to our fathers, ex-husbands, ex-boyfriends, brothers, or uncles. What we should bear in mind when communicating with the men in our lives is *what* we say about men to men. Our men friends sometimes get an ear full of negativity from conversations with us. When they think of their single friends and want to introduce them to someone, we certainly don't come to mind. No one wants to set up a friend with an unhappy person, someone who isn't over her ex, or someone who is negative about men.

If you are overwhelmed with negative feelings regarding men, you will be waiting a long time for one to approach you, for sure. I think some women say they are waiting either because they are tired of trying or in order to run from the responsibility of interaction and engagement with the world in a normal way. I recognize every woman who is single is not entirely to blame for that state of affairs. However, it is not realistic to think that there is no ownership whatsoever.

It can be painful to go year after year and still not realize the dream of having a husband, children, and a family of your own. If you're happy, don't want to marry, and have grown accustomed to living as an independent, single woman, just own your single status and enjoy it instead of playing the blame game. There is nothing wrong with not getting married or not wanting to get married, and it is important to be honest with yourself.

If you do want to be married and have been waiting for a long time, maybe it is time to evaluate what you could be doing. Evaluate your circumstances, just like you would in your career, business, or education. Would you honestly consider *if* you want to be married? If the answer is "yes," then move forward in a positive manner.

Questions to Consider

1. What do you mean when you say you are waiting on the Lord?
2. What ideas, books, and/or speakers have influenced how you think about waiting? Write down those ideas, and prayerfully evaluate their effectiveness in your life. Are they for a teen or young adult? Have the writers changed their minds?
3. What does the Bible say about this subject?
4. What activities are you going to start doing to wait productively?

A friend of mine showed me a post on a social network that said, "Best girlfriend ever." Now this was under a picture of a woman doing the laundry of her boyfriend, who is a known ladies' man. The picture was posted by his single, older sister. If you are catching on to my way of thinking, you know I thought this was ridiculous. I quickly checked to see if the sister was my friend on a social network. She was, so I posted the following: "This is unbelievable! I didn't do Pastor Aaron's laundry until AFTER he married me." After eight or nine other comments, the "girlfriend" posted: "hmmmmmmmmmmmm...... maybe I should change my strategy."

Really? You think so? I think you should too! A perfect segue to the next chapter.

SILLY WOMEN

In some ways, this is a tough chapter to write because we mean well when we do things for the men in our lives. Like the example at the end of the previous chapter, most of the things we do for boyfriends, or for someone we are in a relationship with, are actually husband privileges. As I talk to more women of all ages who are doing these kinds of things, I am beginning to realize this kind of activity is very commonplace. Many women grew up watching unmarried women doing these things for men on a regular basis.

There is not a man alive who wouldn't accept free house-keeping services, childcare, cooking, transportation, and any other service you would like to provide. We view this as a way of showing our love and support. But these things will not keep a marriage together. You can even add sex into the mix, and there is no guarantee there either. All of the above are things we as women can do; however, these things do not make up the essence of who we are, nor do they make us feel valuable and loved.

Now don't get me wrong. When I married my husband, he received an all-access pass to all of those things without restriction. Guess what his all-access pass was? The wedding band he was wearing. He also received an all access pass to who I am as a person and a woman: my spiritual self, intellect, body, unrestricted love, femininity, encouragement, time, attention, and emotional support. Giving a man an all-access pass in any area prior to marriage puts you firmly in the category of "Silly Women."

Trust me when I say I have heard it all:

- You don't know how things have changed.
- You are in for a rude awakening.
- Men expect you to do certain things for them.

I have been told these things by several men.

I know, I know. All three statements are sad but true. Frankly, I have been traumatized by what I have experienced so far as a newly single woman. I'm shocked by how much men have slipped in the basic areas of common courtesy and politeness towards women. Men even treat their women friends poorly. You know why? Because of silly women who have allowed themselves to be treated any kind of way just to have a man or be in a relationship.

This state of affairs makes it difficult for women who respect and value themselves. We women must interact with spoiled, out of practice, relationally lazy, selfish, hot (yes, I said it), very eligible men who are out there looking for the right woman. A woman with values, healthy self-esteem, and a desire for a great man will have to "let patience have its perfect work" (James 1:4).

He Has No Rights

Being patient doesn't mean giving up your life and letting it revolve around a man you are not married to. I am not necessarily an advocate of doing that completely, even after you are married. I have heard there are some men who want to be the focal point of everything in their ladies' lives, but that isn't realistic. What is real is being her priority (after Jesus, of course).

Part of what makes us interesting as women is having outside things we do that make us feel good. We can have activities in our lives that are healthy for us in addition to our relationships with our man and our children. I do not understand involving a man in every important decision of your life when he has

Being patient doesn't mean giving up your life and letting it revolve around a man you are not married to.

no right legally or spiritually to be involved because he is not your husband.

I was meeting with a young woman a few years back, and she was making a decision about college. She said, "I have to talk with my boyfriend about whether I should go to college or just work for now."

My response was, "I don't see why. He doesn't have a say in those types of decisions. He can give his opinion, but that is all it is—an opinion. I know he wants you to care what he thinks, and I am sure you do. However, he is crossing the line and so are you if you allow him to make such an important life decision for you."

I met my husband while we were in college, and we were married two years later. I was pregnant at the beginning of our junior year, and he said he wanted me to quit school. You can probably imagine how that went over with me. I said, "Absolutely not! I came to college to get a degree and not an MRS either. Now I met the man of my dreams and got married, that is a bonus, but I am finishing college, and you are too."

I will admit it was difficult to do with two pregnancies and a husband playing major college basketball; yet, we did it together. (You can take over the world in your twenties.) I never thought I would be on my own and have to support myself and my children. Fortunately, I didn't have to until recently.

Now that I am widow, I am very glad I have my education to fall back on. I was able to get a decent job to take care of myself and not just survive.

While we were in college, I encouraged my husband in his academics and basketball, and he successfully completed both. We graduated together with a three-year-old daughter and two-year-old son, something no one thought we would do.

I share this story with you simply to say that Aaron was my husband, yet I didn't let him dissuade me from something I knew would benefit us both. Nor did I let him dissuade me from fulfilling a lifelong dream of mine to have a college degree. We were both young, nineteen and twenty years old at the time, and were learning how to be married. Note that I said *be married,* not in a relationship. As women, we spend time working at relationships with multiple people we will never marry. There is a difference between learning to get along with someone and developing the skill of compromise.

As women, we spend time working at relationships with multiple people we will never marry.

Spoiled Brats!

To the women in our ranks who have spoiled men who are not their husbands by treating them like their husbands, thanks a lot! I say this for all of the women who want to be married, who recognize that some things are important enough to save for the man who marries you—and not just sex. Silly women deserve all the thanks for turning what could be good, considerate, loyal, faithful, responsible, successful, hard-working, and spiritual men into big, over-grown, spoiled brats! (Whew! I got that off my chest.)

Silly women deserve all the thanks for turning what could be good, considerate, loyal, faithful, responsible, successful, hard-working, and spiritual men into big, over-grown, spoiled brats!

Do you know how difficult it is when there are silly women ready and able to do whatever it takes to keep their men happy—silly women who believe, "He ain't gonna cheat on me!" when he may have cheated on someone to get with you in the first place? Why do you believe that somehow you will be different? If this were true, a whole lot of daytime TV shows would go out of business.

We do not want to be this kind of woman, one willing to do any and everything to get into the good graces of a man who is not her husband. The following scripture from Proverbs describes an enticing woman who is also a married woman, a beautiful example of the misuse of feminine assets. To be a woman who values herself and is valued by men, and treated accordingly, we cannot be like this woman.

[11] She *was* loud and rebellious; her feet would not stay at
home.
[12] At times *she was* outside, at times in the open square,
Lurking at every corner.
[13] So she caught him and kissed him;
With an impudent face she said to him:
[14] "*I have* peace offerings with me; Today I have paid my
vows.
[15] So I came out to meet you, Diligently to seek your face,
And I have found you.
[16] I have spread my bed with tapestry,
Colored coverings of Egyptian linen.
[17] I have perfumed my bed, with myrrh, aloes, and
cinnamon.
[18] Come, let us take our fill of love until morning; Let us
delight ourselves with love.
[19] For my husband *is* not at home;
He has gone on a long journey;
[20] He has taken a bag of money with him,
And will come home on the appointed day."
[21] With her enticing speech she caused him to yield,
With her flattering lips she seduced him.
[22] Immediately he went after her, as an ox goes to the
slaughter,
Or as a fool to the correction of the stocks, [a]
[23] Till an arrow struck his liver. As a bird hastens to the
snare,
He did not know it *would cost* his life.
[24] Now therefore, listen to me, *my* children;
Pay attention to the words of my mouth:
[25] Do not let your heart turn aside to her ways,
Do not stray into her paths;
[26] For she has cast down many wounded,
And all who were slain by her were strong *men*.
[27] Her house *is* the way to hell.

—Proverbs 7:11–27

Cheating Does Not Equal Adultery

I have trouble equating "cheating" while dating with "committing adultery" within a marriage. I understand that if you have agreed to be exclusive with a man, it means you just date each other. If that desire changes for either of you, then you should have the common courtesy to let the other person know. Now this is much easier if neither sex nor heavy petting is involved in the relationship. Know for a fact and accept that if you are not married, you are single. Being a girlfriend is not your greatest accomplishment in life. It is easier to accept that he dates others when you haven't moved in with the man and co-mingled your finances. I am not saying your feelings won't be hurt, because they will be; however, even when you label yourselves as friends, exclusive, courting, and engaged, you are still single.

What a man does when he is single is not necessarily what he will do when he is married. For example, he's much more likely to remain exclusive when the stakes are high (in marriage) and he has something on the line like his money, name, and reputation. Don't kid yourself. Who do you think originated the term "gold digger," a man or a woman? When I was in banking and selling investments, we had a disclosure to clients that went something like this: "Past performance is not always a predictor of future performance." This can be both positive and negative at the same time.

If a man you are or I am dating goes off with some other woman, I would wish him well, if that is what he wanted. Do I consider that cheating? No. He is not my husband. This is just more validation for the title of my book. Come on, say it with me, "Girlfriends don't matter." I get it. When the guy you're dating goes out with another girl, that's painful and maybe a little humiliating, but it doesn't diminish who you are. His actions don't change your value in any way. I truly believe the man God has for me to marry will be right for me. We will share the same values and faith and will be good together. We will make it from friendship to courtship to marriage.

Who knows, that same man who ran off for a minute may come back to me, asking for forgiveness. If he does, the relationship we had has to go up a level; none of this let's-start-over or pick-up-from-where-we-left-off business. That's a NO! The stakes just went up, so come with it! I am worth it!

When we behave like silly women, we come off as naive, at best, desperate and silly at worst. In the book of Proverbs, Bathsheba is giving counsel to her son Solomon. Now remember she was the "other woman" in King David's life (he later married her). She didn't initiate the relationship, but her husband was murdered by the king, she and David then lost their first child together, and the sword never departed from David's home as a result of his sin (see 2 Samuel for the whole story). Years after all these sordid events, Bathsheba is telling her son, "A foolish woman will lead a man to a crust of bread."

She is warning him because she knows there are a group of women out there who don't think of the long-term consequences of their actions to others or even themselves. She also knows the power women have to take a man to the next level, or bring him lower than low. Bathsheba wants Solomon to know that a virtuous woman will take you up, and a foolish or silly woman will take you down.

Bathsheba wants Solomon to know that a virtuous woman will take you up, and a foolish or silly woman will take you down.

It's Just a Piece of Paper

Now I know there are women out there who get whatever they want from their men. If you're one of them, you can manipulate with the best of them and are in control of the relationship. Good for you! The down side to that lifestyle is that when you do want a real relationship, like marriage, you have none of the skills or virtues to make that a reality. Some people naively think that if they live with a man first and do all of the things they should do for a husband, then marriage is just a continuation.

I can tell you from my experience as a pastor, with over twenty years of praying for and helping people, that marriage is not the continuation of doing things for a man who is not your husband. If the wedding and legal paperwork don't change things, why not just get married in the first place? You know why? Because when either of you don't feel like it, get tired of each other, or grow apart, it isn't as simple as packing your bag and leaving. When you are married, you have a legal responsibility—and whether you recognize it or not, a spiritual responsibility—to that person. Guess what, it is called: Commitment=Covenant=Contract.

Contrary to popular belief, most people get married because they really want to, and they do so without a desire to get divorced. They want it to work out. Now if you were unfortunate enough to marry someone or be a person who went into your marriage considering divorce as a possibility, I am sad for you. When you are looking for a way out, you usually find it.

It is a silly concept to look at a non-marriage relationship from the perspective that "so much time has been invested, I want to try and make it work." It is like building on sand instead of a rock. A woman is building a relationship on sand if she's just holding something together because of the time she's spent. An uncommitted relationship is still a bad idea. I have heard

Sometimes it seems that women treat their non-marriage relationships like prison: they are doing time and want credit for time served.

women say, "I've been with him for so long, I can't imagine not being with him," and they are not married. Sometimes it seems that women treat their non-marriage relationships like prison: they are doing time and want credit for time served.

Marriage is not jail if you work at it. It is a wonderful and fulfilling relationship that cannot be approximated, no matter how hard you try (details will be in my next book). If you are content in a non-marriage relationship, then my book isn't written to you specifically. There must be a book out there written about how to live successfully with someone who is not your spouse. But it just isn't healthy to expect spousal privileges when you are not married. Marriage is not just a commitment; it is a covenant. If you are not content in a non-marriage relationship, stop being silly and attempting to apply the rules of marriage when they don't apply.

The Difference Between Wife and Girlfriend

I remember in college when my then boyfriend, Aaron, would want me to wait for him after the basketball games. I just couldn't do it. I felt out of place, waiting with all those women who were hoping one of the guys on the team would pick them up on the way out. It seemed degrading to me. I didn't want to be classified as a loose woman; therefore, I walked home to my dorm. I told Aaron to come by there and pick me up if he wanted to see me.

A couple of years later, when we were married, of course I waited for him after the game. In fact, I walked through the

tunnel to the locker rooms, passed by all of the other girls waiting, sat in the lounge with the coaches' wives, and waited for
my man. I would tell the other girls, "That is the difference
between being a wife and being a girlfriend."

Even though I was only twenty years old at the time, I had
a sense that there were many differences between being married
and not being married. I remember a player being hurt during
one of the games. His girlfriend ran onto the court and was
summarily dismissed by security. This is what I am trying to
help you understand: girlfriends don't matter.

As an older, single woman, holding onto the title of girlfriend is simply silly. Trust me when I say that if a man is not
married, it is because he doesn't want to be married. I get so
tired of hearing excuses about that from men. Too many are
looking for perfection and let the years go by. It is because they
can get their needs met without ever getting married (and not
just sexual needs). This is due to silly women. When the man
gets tired or grows bored with one girlfriend, he dumps her
for another. He then starts the stupid cycle all over again, and
we wonder why there is such a high divorce rate. Men are being trained in the wrong way. They operate by the motto, "If
I get tired or lose interest, I get a new model."

Men are being trained in the wrong way. They operate by the motto, "If I get tired or lose interest, I get a new model."

We are training men to expect everything from us
before they marry us. When they complain, we try to please
them, and when we don't please them, they move on. Men take that same irresponsible
behavior into marriage. What is so amazing to me is that the
next woman thinks she is going to be different somehow. She
is going to play the wifey role even better than the last woman,

and this time, the guy will marry her. I suggest to you that a man won't get married unless he can't get what he wants any other way. This is not meant to be an indictment on men but rather an acknowledgment of the way things are. Wake up, ladies!

Let's Get It Together, Ladies

Recently, I was watching a popular reality TV show in which a woman finally took a stand concerning a man with whom she had a non-marriage relationship. She moved away and began getting herself together, rebuilding her confidence, and working. Guess what happened? The old boyfriend was all in her face when he realized she was willing to move on and have a life without him. She verbalized having higher standards and expectations in the relationship. In other words, she expected fidelity and marriage. One of her so-called friends was even telling her to go back to the guy and accept him no matter what, stating, "It is just who he is." With friends like that, who needs enemies?

Men can change, grow up, and accept responsibility if they want to. Silly women, however, say, "No, let him just be himself: selfish, childish, and irresponsible about your feelings." Really? Is this what we want out of our relationships with men? Of course it isn't.

What man in his right mind doesn't want a confident and secure woman with whom he can build a marriage? I said a man in his right mind, not the kind of man who attempts to get as much as possible from you with the least amount of effort and commitment on his part. I know this flies in the face of what everyone is doing; however, to get out of the category of silly women, you are going to have to make some changes in how you relate to men. I think fear keeps us from taking a ladylike stand because we don't want to lose the man.

Let me give you another example from one of the women
who attended my group. In our first session, I always talk
about the idea that girlfriends don't matter, the list, and the
definition of dating. After my talk and the group discussion,
the ladies have the opportunity to share what they are thinking
and feeling. One lady who was very quiet said she was going
to break it off with her boyfriend as soon as she left my home.
I asked her to take a breath and wait a minute. She needed to
be very sure that's what she wanted to do. This thirty-five-year-
old and her man had been dating about three years, and she
felt the relationship wasn't going anywhere. I warned her to
be prepared for any outcome following that conversation. His
response could be on a scale of 1–10. A "1" = "frankly, my dear,
I don't give a (you know what)," to a "10" = "I can't believe you
are doing this; I wanted to marry you."

She came back to the next session a couple of weeks later
looking absolutely fabulous, happy, and vibrant. I couldn't wait
to ask her what happened. She did exactly what she said she
was going to do and told him she wanted to end the relationship. She said his response was a "3," and he let the relationship
go. There you have it, ladies; he didn't miss a beat and accepted
her decision. OK, everyone say it with me: "Girlfriends don't
matter." Three years of her life just went by in a serial, monogamous relationship with a man who was only a "3" when she
broke it off. Thankfully, she was prepared and able to move on.

You would think that in your thirties and older both men
and women should know what they want in life. It shouldn't
take three years to figure out if you want to marry someone.
Listen to me, ladies! If you want to get married, you cannot tie
your life up for years on end with a man who does not want to
marry you, especially if you want a family.

Maybe you haven't been one of the women to go off the
deep end and be silly about your relationships with men. Yet
you recognize some tendencies from reading this chapter.

When men are ready to build a life, have a family, and go to the next level, they start looking for a next-level woman.

Seriously, if marriage is your goal, you must allow your mind to be renewed in this area. When men are ready to build a life, have a family, and go to the next-level, they start looking for a next level woman. Yes, sometimes they will try to do it with the one they are with; however, change is extremely difficult for some people. They get insecure when a man starts to make his move and sometimes become the girlfriend who didn't matter.

To end this chapter, I have another true story. I have changed some of the facts to protect the identity of the people involved.

This couple dated for five or six years, and the man even moved in with the woman. They were together so long that both families considered them a part of the family. Both families recognized birthdays and celebrated the holidays together. Then the man's family experienced a serious crisis that caused him to stand up and take notice that his life had to change. He was living with his girlfriend, mooching off her, using her credit, and getting high. He had dropped out of college, was inconsistent in his work, and was not being responsible as a man, even though he knew better. After the family crisis, he decided his life was going to have to go through an immediate change.

He began his journey. He got back in school, moved out of his girlfriend's apartment (he didn't end the relationship), went back to his spiritual roots, stopped getting high cold turkey, stepped up on his job, and refinanced his car out of her name. This seems to me to be any woman's dream: her man getting it together and stepping up to the plate. Her response, however, was that of a silly woman.

She didn't like the change. She was comfortable with him being dependent on her financially, estranged from his family, and not serious about his faith. She didn't or couldn't understand the huge impact the family crisis had on his life. For him, it was the "reality check" that he needed. All of the sudden, the old irresponsibility and her providing for him seemed OK to her, until he decided to really be a man.

Do I need to finish this story? He moved on, they broke up. He met someone else and got engaged. She became the classic girlfriend who didn't matter—not because the man didn't want her, but because she didn't want to go to the next level with her man. She wanted to remain a silly woman.

Questions to Consider

1. In what ways have I given in to the new way of having relationships with men?
2. What are the silly woman tendencies in my own life?
3. What changes will I make in my relationships with men?

DESPERATE WANNABE HOUSEWIVES

(This is the chapter about sex before marriage and other ways to give yourself away for free.)

This may be the longest chapter in this book, probably because it could be a book in and of itself. I guess I am passionate about this chapter because I see so many women doing these things over and over again. Furthermore, when the relationship doesn't turn into a marriage and ends, women become hurt. It's not right to go through so much pain over and over again. I know there are women out there who think sex before marriage is necessary and will say I am the one in a fantasy world. In fact, I was told by a male friend of mine, "You are in for a rude awakening. Men aren't going to take you out to lunch, dinner, spend their money, and get nothing from you in return." That is so sad.

My response was, "I don't need a whole lot of men to make the investment in wooing me and respecting my standards; I just need one!"

As if sex, not married lovemaking, is the only benefit of being with me. Come on, men. You know better, or at least you should. Take it from a woman who was married to the same attractive, successful, spiritual man for twenty-nine years. The sex was great, don't get me wrong, but he valued my intelligence, strong character, spirituality, homemaking skills, work ethic, devotion, support, faithfulness to him and our children, and everything else I brought with me to the marriage besides my body.

Another thing single people say is, "You will have to kiss a lot of frogs before you get to the prince." Why would I have to kiss any frogs, especially if I already know they are frogs?

Another thing single people say is, "You will have to kiss a lot of frogs before you get to the prince." Why would I have to kiss any frogs, especially if I already know they are frogs? Let's start using that illusive thing called common sense. I think that statement is just an excuse to knowingly and repeatedly make dumb decisions we know are dumb while we are making them. Stop it! Remember I did say, "No fluffy sugar coating, period."

To Do "IT" or Not to Do "IT," That Is the Question— Sex, That Is!

The first thing we think about when it comes to dating is this: are we going to get into a sexual relationship or not? For some women, it is just a matter of when. I know it is old school not to have sex in a dating relationship. Well, I say, bring back the good ole days and hurry up! I know there has always been sex before marriage; nevertheless, as common as it is now, it is socially, physically (health wise), and emotionally ridiculous.

I have even heard some women say, "What if we are not sexually compatible and I marry him?" I guess that thought never crossed my mind, not even once before I married. This mind-set stems from too many celebrity romances and breakups and TV shows promoting sex outside of marriage and mocking sex inside of marriage. We all get sucked into it. Women have told me, "If I don't sleep with him, he will find someone else." That's true. He will find someone else because there will always be women willing to give their bodies to men for free and for a few I-love-you-babys, you're-my-ladys, or the ever-popular, I-need-this.

Of course, sex is a big thing to both men and women. Any good marriage book will tell you it is and to keep your husband satisfied in this area. Note that I am saying *marriage* book; hence, if you are single, it is not appropriate for you to be meeting this very real need in a man's life—period. If you decide to maintain a biblical standard of no sex before marriage, you had better be ready to be very available to meet your man's needs after you are married. Sex is not a weapon or tool for women to wield, but it is a pleasure to be shared within marriage. Just remember, if he wants *you,* he will respect your boundaries, make the courtship short and sweet, and marry you. You won't have to worry about being a long-term or forever fiancée.

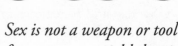

Sex is not a weapon or tool for women to wield, but it is a pleasure to be shared within marriage.

It is also important to note that not having intercourse is simply "technical virginity." We all know that you can go to the moon and back without it.

Sharing this part of yourself with a man you are not married to decreases your self-worth and value in your own eyes. It also makes you accumulate more baggage as you go from one relationship to another. Please note: most men's self-worth will not be impacted one way or another by having premarital sex. Why not reward the man who makes the real commitment to you and marries you with your body being solely his?

Now I realize a lot of women reading this book may already be active sexually. Well, if you are not married, stop it! You can do it and will be amazed at how your self-esteem increases, your confidence emerges, and you start to get the respect you deserve. Of course, the men will say, "Are you serious?" Some won't want to date you because you are not "giving it up." Just remember this: the man who marries you will be glad he doesn't have to look in the face of numerous men who know your body as intimately as he does.

I don't know why this is even an issue for argument within church circles, but it is. I know people who go to church every Sunday and sometimes mid-week services too, believe in Jesus, are saved, and yet will argue, "You need to 'try it,' before you 'buy it.'" Some say it is a matter of conscious and should not be hard and fast criteria. I understand the idea of biblical mandates, community standards, and personal convictions. I'd say that not having premarital sex clearly falls in all three categories for me, and the first category for everyone who is a Christian. I also hear that the premarital sex question could be your personal conviction to do it anyway. We all have free will. But I would challenge you: if you are a Christian, pray for real for clarity before you make a final decision on this one.

Even though this book is written to women, I know there will be men reading it too. I want you to know that men are not exempt from what I am saying here about sex. If a man does meet a woman he wants who adheres to the "no sex before marriage" criteria, he will have to, by default, clean up his own act. I am not so naive to think men and women, Christian or not, are not having sex. Just remember, everybody isn't doing it, no matter what you hear or see on TV. Remember what your parents used to say: "If all your friends decide to climb the Space Needle and jump off the top, are you going to jump just because they did it?" Of course I am exaggerating to make the point that everybody isn't doing it. And even if they are, so what? Be your own person; make good choices.

One last thing, with regard to the sex issue. My children would ask me for advice about how to handle relational, work-related, or any kind of problem in which they were do-ing things that were contrary to what their father and I had taught them. My response was, "It is very difficult for me to give you good counsel when you are operating out-side of the realm in which I have experience." Now I did my best to help them based on sound principles and good judgment, but I would warn them, "When you violate principles, you cannot expect good to come from it."

"When you violate prin-ciples, you cannot expect good to come from it."

Stop the Drama, Please!

Another big area where we give ourselves away is emotion-ally. Women are not the only ones with drama and emotional problems and issues. Be careful with this one; tread very care-fully. I know you want to "be there" for your man. Please let me say this: First, he is not *your* man because he is not your husband. Secondly, it is not your responsibility to give yourself to a man who is not your husband.

I am not saying you are not to be supportive and encourag-ing. As a single man or woman, you should have an emotional support system, one that includes friends, family, co-workers, and colleagues. You need people who can be there for you in appropriate ways when you need emotional support. But until you have a spouse, you don't experience the most intimate level of relational support. This is what makes marriage so special and unique: the whole mystery of the two becoming one.

I understand the difference personally. The deep emotional intimacy and support that only the marriage covenant can provide—oh, how I miss it. However, I recognize that it would be inappropriate for me to put the weight of that responsibility on a man who is not my husband, no matter how capable or willing he may be. Furthermore, it is equally inappropriate for a man to expect a woman who is not his wife to jump on his emotional ride. There is openness and vulnerability required that is high-risk outside of marriage. Just ask some ex-girlfriends you know; they will tell you that they are still trying to recover from doing the very thing I am describing here.

To be supportive, you can listen and say, for example: "I hope you feel better." "Do you have some male friends who can help?" "Have you talked with your family?" "Do you have a pastor or mentor?" When you are his friend or the woman he is seeing exclusively, his emotional well-being is not your responsibility.

Here is an example: If a man has roller-coaster emotional needs, as his wife, you would need to get on and ride with him. If you are not his wife, you need to stand at the bottom and tell him, "There are turns coming." Encourage his friends to be supportive, recommend a counselor if needed, tell him it's almost over, and wait patiently for him to get off. Then congratulate him for weathering the storm and winning. This is what you would do for any friend, male or female, and a mature person would value your support and thank you for it.

Because of our caring, nurturing nature as women, we take on far more than we should in our relationships with men outside of marriage. Some men will say, "I want a woman who has

Women make so many sacrifices and give in ways we should reserve for the only man who deserves it, our husband.

my back." If that is true, then he will honor her and marry her, and she will have his sides and front as well. Women make so many sacrifices and give in ways we should reserve for the only man who deserves it, our husband.

Another area we give to men before marriage is having their children. I know this is a touchy subject because some pregnancies are unplanned, and we keep our children (may God bless you abundantly for that). What I am talking about are women who actually believe that having a child with a man somehow equates to having a child with your husband. When you are not married, a man has no obligation to you, period, not in any way—emotionally, financially, educationally, or relationally. However, he does have obligations in all of the above areas for his child or children. If your non-marriage relationship with him ends, the only responsibility he has is to his children. (I am not a lawyer, so don't get technical on me. You know what I am trying to say here.)

My mom told my sisters and me, "If you play house, you will never have a home." It is a scary thought that we do a man the honor of having his child, lose our figures (at least for a while), give up sleep, breast-feed, and basically forego the next eighteen–twenty-five years of our freedom. He is not our husband and he may not stick around to help. Ladies, we certainly need to evaluate this lifestyle choice we are making, not just for ourselves but also for our children.

I applaud all of the good men out there who step up and marry women who already have children due to being widowed, divorced, or never married. (Kudos to my son-in-law.) They are to be commended for loving a woman and her kids and for being a husband and stepping up as a father. If you don't have children, please hear me when I say that a man should marry you if he wants you to have his children. Yes, I said it! OK, are you tired of me yet?

Money, Money, Money, Money ... Money!

> Do not lay up for yourselves treasures on earth, where moth and rust destroy and where thieves break in and steal; but lay up for yourselves treasures in heaven, where neither moth nor rust destroys and where thieves do not break in and steal. For where your treasure is, there your heart will be also.
>
> —Matthew 6:19–21

Why in the world do we share our financial resources with men we are not married to? I have heard some of the most amazing things like, "His car broke down, and he couldn't get to work, so I let him use mine." Are you serious? Let's talk about who is going to be financially responsible if he gets in an accident in your car. YOU! That is who! Don't you remember when your parents told you that you couldn't drive their car because you weren't on the insurance? You do not have to prove you care about a man by letting him have access

You do not have to prove you care about a man by letting him have access to your personal property and finances, especially if he is not your husband.

to your personal property and finances, especially if he is not your husband.

I would prefer a man I date to have his own car, his own place to live, and friends who can help him out in a bind. I am not saying you can't give him a ride to work once in a while, while *he* is paying for his car to get fixed.

Oh and I heard a "girlfriend" say, "He's about to get evicted and needs somewhere to stay until he finds a place." Well, if his friends and family turned him down as a tenant, you should too, if he even asked them. I am not saying people don't fall on hard times, but as a non-wife, it is not your responsibility to help. I know there are a lot of men just trying to make it. If that is the case, they probably should be focusing on that 100% and not dating you.

Trust me, once you are married, you will have ample opportunity to stand by, support, love, and help your man in good times and bad. To do it before you are married? Wow! You will be jaded and bitter. When your husband finally does come along, you will be telling him what you aren't going to do because you used up all of your freshness and energy doling out husband privileges when you were a girlfriend.

I started this section with a scripture, "Where your treasure is, there your heart will be also" (Matthew 6:21). Proverbs 4:23 says, "Keep your heart with all diligence, for out of it spring the issues of life." This is why we are so tied to men when we get involved with them financially. We pay their bills, bail them out of jail, pay tuition and childcare for their children, cook dinner, and let them live with us.

A Different Take on Intellectual Property

And remain in the same house, eating and drinking such things as they give, for the laborer is worthy of his wages …
—Luke 10:7

It may be difficult to believe, but the investments you have made in your education, in learning different skills, and in gaining other experiences are valuable commodities. You should place great value and significance on these in your life. I have heard stories of girlfriends doing term papers, completing homework assignments, and even taking entire online classes on behalf of their boyfriends. Women, as girlfriends, help men with their businesses by being bookkeepers, working for free, volunteering at their events, and setting up websites. While the desire to help someone in need is admirable, it is intellectually irresponsible. How can you ever expect to get paid to do something you so willingly give away for free?

Your natural and learned intellectual skills are just a small part of the very important things you bring to the table when you get married. These skills should be valued as the precious gems they are. Not just your degree, but your

After giving so much of themselves, it is no wonder so many women are devastated when a non-marriage relationship ends.

natural common sense, intuitiveness, and knack for living life well are assets you bring to the table. After giving so much of themselves, it is no wonder so many women are devastated when a non-marriage relationship ends. You need to learn as a woman how to give a good sneak preview; however, he has to go to the movie to see the whole picture. Now I am talking about previews that live up to the movie; don't misrepresent yourself. Misrepresentation will only hurt you and break down trust in your marriage in the end.

I owned and operated a custom sewing and alterations business for eight years while my children were small. I custom made wedding gowns and formal wear and did alterations on clothing. I remember investing my own money, and my husband's godparents gave me ten thousand dollar to get the business going. I recall friends asking me for a discount or, worse yet, free services. Thank God I had my degree in business, and I knew I would never make any money starting out with customers who didn't want to pay for the services I was providing.

No matter what our skill set is, there is someone out there who is willing to pay us to utilize it or get our advice. Yes, there are working mothers, executives, and families who would pay you good money to put a hot, healthy, home-cooked meal on their table every night, or do laundry, housekeeping, tax counseling, or tutoring. This may sound pretty hard core, but I even try to stick to this policy with friends. There is nothing worse than spending three–four hours of your time with someone, giving your best counsel and advice for free, and then he or she turns around and does the opposite. Now if someone is paying me a consulting fee per hour and then chooses not to take my advice, I don't give it a second thought.

My point is that if you give your intellectual property away for free with a man you are not married to, don't expect him to value it much, even if he uses it and has success as result. When you break-up, he may take all of the credit for himself. When you are married, this doesn't matter because you are one. His success is your success and vice versa.

Just think about it: you invested two–eight years of your life getting an education, earning your A.A., B.A., M.A., and/ or Ph.D., spent thousands of dollars (and you still may be paying on school loans), and every man who wants to make you his girlfriend gets to use it? I don't think so! Now, if I am asked for my opinion on something, or to read something and say what I think, I will do it. But here is the catch: he will get a limited response, and I will tell a man honestly why. "I am a widow. I have to take care of myself, and I must make sure I leave an inheritance for my children's children; therefore, I don't usually consult with anyone for free, not even my own family members."

Another True Story

I went to visit my younger son, who is in a business that requires continuous training and development. He has not finished his B.A. in business yet, and he wanted me to sit in on the day-long training to give my assessment and critique. He did an amazing job and is naturally gifted at leadership and training. Yes, I am a proud mother! At the end of the day, he asked me what I thought about his training. I recommended he develop a manual containing the information. The new employees could then write down specifics and notes and highlight what they needed rather than trying to write down every word he was saying. The manual could also serve as a guide everyday for his team when he is not around to answer questions. I gave him five or six other pointers before I returned home. See, I am not giving away my skills in my own book either.

A couple of months later, he called me to say he had completed his training manual, implemented my other suggestions, and also made some videos to go with it and a "Train the Trainer" manual.

This is just one example of my new take on intellectual property. Yes, I do have a B.A. and M.B.A. and over twenty-five years of work experience, and my son got that for free, my late husband got that for free, my daughter and grand kids get it for free, but a boyfriend? NO. That consulting will be $175 per hour, please (with a smile, of course).

The Spirit Is So Willing

> Watch and pray, lest you enter into temptation. The spirit indeed is willing, but the flesh is weak.
> —Mark 14:38

A final way we give ourselves away to men in non-marriage relationships is spiritually. All of us are a three-part being:

spirit, soul, and body. The areas I have covered in this chapter are related to soul and body, but now to the most critical part, in my view, the spirit. We can bond to a person on three levels, and that is meant to happen between a man and a woman in the covenant of marriage. They are to become one. Having personally experienced this, I know how absolutely wonderful it is and how intimate, and at times painful, it can be. The price is complete vulnerability to the other person. This is too high a price to pay with someone you are not married to, someone who did not promise you "for better or worse, sickness and in health, forsaking all others, until death do you part."

I have lived out and fulfilled all of these vows all the way to the end, through doing CPR, through planning a burial and memorial service, through speaking about and honoring my late husband for the last time, through helping my children and grandchildren through the first year after his death, and through a lifetime commitment of honoring his contribution to my life and his memory. My life was spiritually connected to my late husband. Why? Because we prayed together, joined our lives in the sight of God and witnesses together, fasted together, read the Word together, and worshiped together. All of these

activities create a bond that ties you to another person spiritually.

When you yield yourself spiritually to a man who is not your husband, you are not more protected, you are actually more vulnerable.

Spiritual bonds will also happen within prayer groups or with friends you pray with on a regular basis. You get to know a person in a spiritual way. This isn't bad at all; you just need to have proper boundaries when praying with someone. When you yield

yourself spiritually to a man who is not your husband, you are not more protected, you are actually more vulnerable. It is no different than going to a church where you know the pastor is stealing from the church or cheating on his wife. When you expose yourself to someone spiritually, you open yourself up in a way that can bring things into your life you did not intend.

So what do I mean by giving yourself away spiritually? You do this by taking the responsibility of his spirituality on yourself. You pester or ask him continually about going to church. You make it your mission to make sure he understands what you believe. You insist on having prayer times together on a regular basis, asking him how you can pray for him, his children, his job, his family, and then telling him how "he is always in your prayers." You do all of this unsolicited by him, not at his request on occasion, but you take it on as your mission to cover him in prayer because, of course, he may be "the one."

None of this is your responsibility, your job, or a way for you to prove you are committed. What is interesting is that so many women will get spiritually involved before marriage, and after they are married, they completely stop. I guess they got what they wanted, so they are ready to coast. After marriage, they start going to women's conferences, buying books on how to pray for their husbands, and more books on how to pray with him.

Do yourself a favor, and save all of your spiritual energy for your marriage. Don't waste it on man after man you will never marry. I am not saying you shouldn't pray for a man. Just keep him in the same category of how you pray for

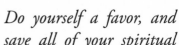

Do yourself a favor, and save all of your spiritual energy for your marriage.

your friends, someone at church who comes forward for prayer, or a complete stranger. Besides, most praying prior to marriage, if you don't have the right mind-set, is to fix the man and to get what you want. Tell the truth, and shame the devil!

OK, so there may be a few of you out there who are pure in every thought and sincerely just want to pray for him. I have one question, no actually three questions: Would you pray for him if he were just a friend? Will you still be praying for him when he breaks up with you (good prayers, not curses)? If you part ways, will you even be speaking to him at all, let alone praying for him? Let's get real here.

If you are fighting me on this right now, go ahead. You bought this book for a reason, maybe just to see what I had to say. Maybe you are married and wanted to see if there was anything you could use (I am sure there is), or you are tired of doing the same thing the same way, expecting different results, and are ready to change. If it is the latter, believe me when I say that you don't want to go too far spiritually with a man you are not married to.

What if he is my prayer partner? Why do you have a man as your primary prayer partner, especially one with which you could have a romantic interest. Really? Trust me, I wouldn't be writing this if I hadn't heard it from real people. If you want a way around this, you will find it.

So now you ask, "What am I supposed to do, then?" First, you should pray for the will of God in your life, especially regarding any dating relationship(s) you are in. Pray for discernment to know why this person has crossed your path: for a reason, for a season, for friendship, or for life. If you are a Christian, you know Jesus is specific when He answers our prayers, and His answers are never contrary to His Word. I am just now feeling ready to venture into the dating world again after being a widow for a little over two years. There is a difference between understanding a person's beliefs about God, Jesus, and faith and getting involved with him spiritually.

There is a difference between understanding a person's beliefs about God, Jesus, and faith and getting involved with him spiritually.

Over the course of time, watch what people do, how they respond to blessings and adversity, and you will learn a lot. What observation doesn't bring out, a few candid conversations will. Can we be honest here? We know praying with people connects them to us and us to them. Don't use this in a dating relationship to attempt to get what you want under the guise of being spiritual. This will backfire on you. It is simple to change, but it is not easy. Just stop, check your motives, and then proceed with caution.

I want to end this chapter with a word of encouragement from the second chapter of Corinthians in the Bible. I said I would be going counter to the culture of our day and what even some leading experts, celebrities, and reality TV shows are portraying about relationships.

I firmly believe the only and best authority on relationships is God himself. He made the ultimate sacrifice in sending His only Son to save the world. He created us for relationship: first with Him and then with each other. He shows us in His Word (the Bible) the ups and downs of relationships, great examples of what we should do and what we should not do, stories of betrayal, how we should live this life, and ultimate, unconditional love. Be encouraged, you are valuable; you can be successful in relationships when Jesus is your guide.

I close this chapter with 2 Corinthians 6:1–18 from the Message Bible:

> Companions as we are in this work with you, we beg you,
> please don't squander one bit of this marvelous life God has

given us. God reminds us, I heard your call in the nick of time; the day you needed me, I was there to help.

Well, now is the right time to listen, the day to be helped. Don't put it off; don't frustrate God's work by showing up late, throwing a question mark over everything we're doing. Our work as God's servants gets validated—or not—in the details. People are watching us as we stay at our post, alertly, unswervingly ... in hard times, tough times, bad times; when we're beaten up, jailed, and mobbed; working hard, working late, working without eating; with pure heart, clear head, steady hand; in gentleness, holiness, and honest love; when we're telling the truth, and when God's showing his power; when we're doing our best setting things right; when we're praised, and when we're blamed; slandered, and honored; true to our word, though distrusted; ignored by the world, but recognized by God; terrifically alive, though rumored to be dead; beaten within an inch of our lives, but refusing to die; immersed in tears, yet always filled with deep joy; living on handouts, yet enriching many; having nothing, having it all.

Dear, dear Corinthians, I can't tell you how much I long for you to enter this wide-open, spacious life. We didn't fence you in. The smallness you feel comes from within you. Your lives aren't small, but you're living them in a small way. I'm speaking as plainly as I can and with great affection. Open up your lives. Live openly and expansively!

Don't become partners with those who reject God. How can you make a partnership out of right and wrong? That's not partnership; that's war. Is light best friends with the dark? Does Christ go strolling with the Devil? Do trust and mistrust hold hands? Who would think of setting up pagan idols in God's holy Temple? But that is exactly what we are, each of us a temple in whom God lives. God himself put it this way:

"I'll live in them, move into them;
I'll be their God and they'll be my people.
So leave the corruption and compromise;
leave it for good," says God.
"Don't link up with those who will pollute you.
I want you all for myself.
I'll be a Father to you;
you'll be sons and daughters to me."
The Word of the Master, God.

Questions to Consider:

1. Which three areas in this chapter present the biggest challenge to you?
2. Which area(s) are you willing to change in the next ninety days?
3. Who will you ask to be a mentor in your life to help you make better decisions and follow through?

8

YOU ARE NOT
A CELEBRITY

Ladies, this is where we need a wake up call. I watch a few of the reality TV shows, and they are not, I repeat, not the real world for most of us, thank God. When we try to emulate the people we see on TV or in the limelight, we devastate our own sense of worth, value, and self-esteem, and we don't have the excess cash flow to cover it up. We live in a world that can make you famous overnight for the silliest and most vulgar reasons. Contrast that with how Webster's Dictionary defines "celebrity" and being famous:

> Celebrity: the state of being celebrated, a famous or celebrated person
> Famous: widely known, honored for achievement

Both definitions deliver a positive connotation and a desirable flavor. However, we know that in the last fifteen years, people can become either celebrities or infamous from a video-sharing site, micro blogging, or a super popular social media network fan page because they were made a fool of or did something really stupid. You may live in a city where the man you are dating is known because of his community involvement, elected office, or athletic accomplishments. He may be a church pastor, business executive, music promoter, or TV personality.

That man may be a celebrity, and therefore, he's accustomed to getting his way, being catered to, and ignoring the feelings of others. He actually may be a pretty selfish person. This doesn't mean he hasn't learned to be accommodating and personable in his business pursuits, or he wouldn't be successful. However, if you cater to this behavior in your personal relationship with a man like this, more than likely you will end up unhappy, taken advantage of, and with low self-esteem. There is a difference between respecting a person's accomplishments and tolerating rude, unacceptable, demeaning behavior. Disrespect is a high price to pay for designer clothes, access to events, envy, and mistreatment by other women.

There is a difference between respecting a person's accomplishments and tolerating rude, unacceptable, demeaning behavior.

Celebrity Tendencies Defined

Women and men can craft an image of themselves to portray to the world that is not reflective of who they really are. The image they create is not sustainable long term and must be maintained and fed. The best way to describe this strategy is in a physical way, whether it's hairstyling with weaves, extensions, or infusions; wearing designer clothing, bags, shoes, and jewelry; attending certain events; or affecting a personality thought to be more appealing to a man or a social group being targeted. This image crafting can clearly be seen in the world of professional sports, in the music industry, and even in church.

You don't have to be famous to act like you are. This play-acting is achieved by treating people as if they were irrelevant and unimportant, by not answering your phone, or by neglecting to return calls and e-mails. You are busy social networking your life like everyone wants to know your every thought and action.

When it comes to relationships, if you want marriage, acting like a celebrity will make success difficult. You would think a high-achieving man would want a high-achieving woman. Sadly, some of these men are just as insecure as we are, and they wonder if anyone would love them if they weren't famous. Some high-achieving men will go after the kind of woman who will just be there for them, has no dreams of her own, has his kids, has sex, and stays skinny and good looking. You know the drill. Who wants to do only that? A marriage should be that and more.

Sometimes the way a celebrity mind-set manifests itself in our lives is in how we segregate or isolate ourselves from or elevate ourselves above certain men. We do this because of their education level, where they were raised, their ethnicity, their job classifications, how much money they make, the cars they drive, the ways they dress or talk, or how many children they have. What if someone were to take a snapshot of you and classify you based on all these things, locking you in for the rest of your life? Is that what you want? Yet we judge in this way continually while dating, and then we wonder why we go from one relationship to another, remaining single and unable to find anyone. What about what is going on inside a man's head? Are we even concerned at all about his goals, dreams, and aspirations in life? Just remember that a very wealthy, celebrity type man may not be planning at all and may just be living it up.

Chemistry and sparks may be immediate or may develop over time, but being impatient and thinking everything is instant may cause you to miss out on your prince charming.

Having a celebrity mindset can cause us to see how we can use a man rather than how we can complete each other or work and build together. This

mindset brings you into a relationship based on these questions: "What can I do for him?" "How can he get me to the next level?"

Where is the spark? I have to have chemistry. Chemistry and sparks may be immediate or may develop over time, but being impatient and thinking everything is instant may cause you to miss out on your prince charming. You will have chemistry and sparks with a lot of men, but that doesn't mean you should have sex with them or marry them.

Look at the chart below. Place a check next to the words or phrases that best describe how you function in your relationships with men. Think about it.

Celebrity Mindset	Relational Mindset
☐ Selfish	☐ Always try to look your best
☐ Appearance is everything	☐ Considerate of others time
☐ Everything by your schedule	☐ Clear in your communication
☐ Don't answer your calls	☐ On time
☐ Don't reply in a timely manner	☐ Value friendship
☐ Do things at the last minute	☐ Answer your own phone
☐ Always go out with an entourage	☐ Communicate verbally and in person as much as possible
☐ Rely on texting and micro blogging to communicate	☐ Willing to spend one-on-one time
☐ Only socialize with those of a certain economic/social class	☐ Willing to date different types of men
☐ Only date one type of man (you have a detailed description)	☐ Like brands but don't flaunt
☐ Show up late	☐ Will compromise with scheduling dates/events
☐ Must look a certain way (will do whatever it takes to achieve this look)	☐ Flexible when needed
	☐ Exercise discretion with social media
☐ Only wear certain brands	☐ Socialize with a wide variety of people
☐ Post on social networking sites irrelevant details about your life	
☐ Only interested in wealthy men	☐ Allow the man to pursue, then you respond

Fantasy Man

I watched a movie in which one of the female character's whole goal in life was to get a certain type of man. She diligently studied what type of woman he would prefer, as if it were a college course. Oh yes, she succeeded in getting him— at the expense of one of her very best friends. Then when his celebrity status was threatened by injury, she dumped him. The best part of the movie happened when he recovered from his injury, tried to work it out with the girlfriend, but eventually moved on when he recognized that she was insincere and phony. He later started dating a woman who appreciated him for who he was without his celebrity status, was his friend already, and was confident in herself. They ended up together and married in the movie.

There comes a time when the fame fades, disappointments and setbacks happen in life, and couples are forced to ask the question, "What do we really have here?" We see these conversations, adulteries, and breakups on public display in the tabloids and newspapers all the time.

Some may say, "Hey, I'd rather have a celebrity-like relationship for a season than never be married or be with a poor man or lead a boring single life." Take it from someone who was married for almost three decades: there's nothing like being in a marriage with a man who just plain loves you. Good, bad, or ugly, he cares about you, invests in you, and encourages and prays for you; and you do the same for him. That is what makes a marriage a relationship. It is not things and money; although, they do enhance it. It is sad to see how much women are willing to give up in order to get "things" in this life. Things that can be stolen, destroyed, used up, and abandoned.

> For what profit is it to a man [woman] if he [she] gains the whole world, and loses his [her] own soul? Or what will a man [woman] give in exchange for his [her] soul?
> —Matthew 16:26

I can tell you from my own personal experience that when I watched my husband take his last breaths, what mattered to me was the bond that we had with one another spiritually, physically, and emotionally. He was a man of stature, well respected and well known in the community in which we lived. We had achieved a good level of success, had purchased a nice home, and had raised our children. We were living our dreams in so many ways, having that special time together and really enjoying each another. Intimacy is what mattered in the end. When the hard things in life happened, "things" become irrelevant. This fact is played out every single day in the news. Things don't matter in the wake and devastation of a failed relationship.

While seeking the celebrity-like one in a million, or the fantasy man we have been dreaming about for years, we may be overlooking our prince charming who is sitting right in front of us. Women spend time talking to their male friends and telling them about how hard it is to get a date or to find someone to love. We whine and complain while he sits patiently listening, empathizing, and handing us tissues when we start crying. All the while, we are looking right past him. Here's a guy who listens to you, answers his phone in the middle of the night because some other guy just dumped you, and is obviously someone whose opinion you value. Take a step back. Take a look at the men in your life who may have escaped your notice because of a celebrity mentality. Do you think fame or status is enough on which to build a marriage?

Learn to See Potential

> For I say, through the grace given to me, to everyone who is among you, not to think of himself [herself] more highly than he [she] ought to think, but to think soberly, as God has dealt to each one a measure of faith.
>
> —Romans 12:3

When humility and genuine care and kindness for others are missing, we will overlook wonderful men in our lives and the treasures right in front of our faces. I see this a lot with all ages of women, especially with the younger ones. It is a known fact that boys develop more slowly than girls, from the time they are born until they are adults. It amazes me that we forget this when we are dating and have expectations that probably won't be met for years by the men we date and eventually marry. This is especially true of men, in their late teens to early thirties. There are some very mature younger men, but they are the 20 percent of men, not the 80 percent.

There is a picture of my late husband hanging in the main hallway of Mount Tahoma High School in Tacoma, Washington. He was inducted into the Hall of Fame in 2006. The plaque includes a picture from when he was in his late thirties and his high school picture from his senior year. I met him freshman year of college, so he looked like his high school picture. I told him many times after he reached his late twenties that if I had a choice of him at twenty (when we married) or thirty, I would have definitely picked the thirty-year-old. Men are like a good wine, they definitely get better with age. He was a great guy at twenty, but at thirty, forty, and even at the time of his death, he just kept getting better and better. I saw his potential, character, life goals, and dreams, and I knew we could do great things together.

Speaking of high school, our daughter told both of us that we were lucky we never had to look back at our high school pictures and say, "I wish I still looked like I did in high school," because we looked better now. We always had a good laugh about that one because it was true.

Let's face it, the average woman doesn't have the financial resources for beauty treatments, weaves or hair extensions, liposuction, breast implants, and lashes so that we can impress the celebrity type men with our appearance. However, we can do our own hair and put our best foot forward, knowing that the combination of body, soul, and spirit gives us something great to offer as a woman and as a wife.

I know there are women reading this book who don't care one way or the other about what I'm saying because their life mission is to lend their energy and talents to making themselves look as good as they possibly can in the hopes of capturing a rich, powerful, good-looking guy. Do your thing, and good luck. *Girlfriends Don't Matter* is not for the 10 percent on either end of the bell curve; it is for 80 percent of women and even

men who want to have a good life and find the fulfillment only
a good marriage can bring.

There are single men out there who have never been married, widowed, or divorced, who are just as disillusioned and
disappointed as we are with the state of affairs when it comes
to finding a partner in life. I
had a man recently ask me,
when I was telling him about
this book, if I thought that the
majority of women would buy
into the idea that they are not
competing with other women.
Would they understand or
accept that if a man wants
another woman, that is not
a slight to them personally. I
agree with him that it is difficult to change the perceptions

*Nothing is more attractive
in women than confidence,
true spirituality, respect,
and a well-kept appearance.*

of people, but you have to believe in yourself. If you don't, no
one else will. Nothing is more attractive in women than confidence, true spirituality, respect, and a well-kept appearance.
These are characteristics we should want, whether we have a
man in our lives or not.

You do not have to buy the lie that in order to be in a
relationship with a man, you must be reduced to a beck-and-
call girl, have low self-esteem, be treated with disrespect and
thoughtless behavior, settle for being a long-time girlfriend,
and constantly try to live up to perfection. Unfortunately, we
see this everyday in so-called "relationships" between celebrities. These degrading relationships are ridiculous, demeaning,
selfish, self-centered, painful, and demoralizing for women and
the men they are dealing with. Yes, I said it, someone had to!
That's the bad news.

Now, here is the good news: You are not a celebrity! You
don't have to live that way. You can be empowered, encouraged, and equipped to lead a healthy, vibrant life emotionally,
spiritually, and physically in the area of your relationships with
men and be found by that special someone.

Questions to Consider

1. How have you acted like a celebrity in your relationships?
2. What types of behaviors do you accept from men that you
   should not accept?
3. How has this behavior hurt your relationships?
4. Do real-life celebrities and their relationships affect how
   you approach dating, courtship, and marriage? If so, how?
   If not, why not?
5. What steps do you plan to take to be your best you?

SECTION THREE

NEW NORMS

Congratulations on getting this far! These last four chapters will answer the question, "What should I be thinking?" In this section, we will look at the process of how you can begin to move forward. So get ready to build up, be inspired, and be encouraged. Some things you believe will be reinforced, others will be challenged, or you may flat disagree with me on others. It is all OK and part of the process. Get ready to build up, to laugh, and to dance. Here we go—again!

> A time to break down,
> And a time to build up;
> A time to weep,
> And a time to laugh;
> A time to mourn,
> And a time to dance …
> —Ecclesiastes 3:3–4 KJV

9

FRIENDSHIP LEADS TO COURTSHIP; COURTSHIP LEADS TO MARRIAGE

I know you have been waiting for this chapter, and it is not exactly what you think. We all hear people say, "I married my best friend." I love to hear that because we all aspire to marry someone we feel knows us well and whom we know well. We know how he reacts under pressure and while having fun. I am not referring to the idea of going through the four seasons with him. (Dating someone through spring, summer, winter and fall to see how they react to life.) This book is directed towards women who have an understanding about how to let a relationship develop. There isn't a formula or a one-size-fits-all; but ending up with a great relationship will require us to get to know ourselves and what we want and be faith-filled and wise in our approach.

Friendship

While you are getting to know men, you should get to know a lot of them as friends. This is true dating. Let go of the mindset of serial, monogamous relationships with men until you get to courtship and marriage. If you want to know men, spend platonic time with them. You certainly can do that with more than one man at a time.

I have found that a man I am really interested in doesn't want to get to know me in a normal way. I believe it is because the physical, romantic piece is off the table. It is so obvious that he is not used to that. The other option that is always on the table is for him to say that he is just not interested.

When I speak about friendship, I mean no sticking your tongue down each other's throats or "watching movies" together, which is code for making out or having sex. When you remove this from your dating relationships, you will get to know the men you date much better. You will also have no guilt or condemnation about seeing many different people at the same time.

You will also learn if a man wants to get to know you as a person or if he just wants sex. All men want sex; that is normal. Now don't get worried about what people think or that your friends will think you are a beck-and-call girl. Trust me on this: if you are a beck-and-call girl and you are sleeping around with lots of men, everyone will know it; and if you aren't sleeping around, everyone will know it. The Bible says, "The fear of man brings a snare" (Proverbs

You could have dated the last three men who took up nine years of your life at the same time and found out within six months that none of them were for you.

29:25). I wonder what everyone thinks about your being in one serial, monogamous dating relationship after another and still no wedding. You could have dated the last three men who took up nine years of your life at the same time and found out within six months that none of them were for you.

I know the idea of not having sex in a relationship is a tough pill to swallow in this day and age. You may even be laughing out loud right now, just at the thought of my saying something that old school. You may even think it is out of fashion. I'm saying it. The reason I'm saying it is because having sex isn't getting women closer to being married. I'm not sure why we can't learn how to have friendships with men. Of course men want more; they always do. It is normal and natural, but there is a time and place, after marriage, and you can have all you want. However, be prepared to deliver on your promise.

When you are married, a lot of your friends are also married couples, so it certainly has been an adjustment for me to now be single. It doesn't help either when my adult children tell me that no man wants to be my "friend." I had a single, male friend tell me that what they said is true: that a man may accept friendship if that is all he thinks he can have but will go for more if the lady says so. I think men are as adverse to rejection as we are and that they think twice before approaching a woman, even if she does send all the right signals. Men are amazing and interesting and a lot of fun, even as just friends. You will get to know them so much better the longer you can keep it that way.

The kind of friendship I am advocating is a non-sexual friendship: no friends with benefits; rather, the benefit of your company and conversation only. The redefinition of terms is making the process of finding the one we love so hard, and it doesn't need to be. Many terms have been redefined, and certainly, the term *friendship* is one of them. In fact, friendship has been portrayed as dumb or immature and not as something in which cool, modern, socially savvy people participate. Honestly, being able to relate to a man, spend time with him, and enjoy his company without any of the physical or sexual overtones is a lost art.

Honestly, being able to relate to a man, spend time with him, and enjoy his company without any of the physical or sexual overtones is a lost art.

One of the questions I ask the ladies in my single women's groups is, "Do you know when a man is attracted or interested in you, or both?"

They all admit they do eventually. I do admit that it is difficult to know, especially when the man doesn't say something to you and is very guarded with his feelings. I am not in denial that while you are being friends you can experience attraction. The longer you keep the physical aspects of the relationship out, the better you will get to know each other (this includes not holding hands and kissing). Most men want physical contact, and you must use good judgment and treat men as individuals.

The transition from friendship to courtship is not easy. For one person involved, it literally could have been love at first sight. For the other, it may have taken time to consider the other person as a long-term partner for marriage. At some point, both people get to the same place. Then there's that awkward moment when they ask the question, "How do we move this to the next level?" I think it is especially difficult if you have a twenty-first century, serial-monogamous-relationship view of dating.

What I'm promoting is for you to view dating as friendship, allowing yourself to build several friendships with men at one time. Then you wake up one morning and realize that one man stands out from the others, and you wonder if he feels the same way about you. It is so important during the friendship stage to be honest with the men you are dating and tell them you are dating other men too.

My first date in thirty-one years was with a man much younger than I am. I went for a couple of reasons: 1) he was persistent and kept asking, and 2) I wanted to ask him what a young man like him wanted with a woman old enough to be his mother. On one hand, it is flattering that a much younger man was interested, or at least, thought he was; however, I am a realist and knew in the long run it wouldn't be good for either of us.

This young man was a little put off that I wasn't just dating him (which I think is typical of most men in today's society). I found it totally shocking that someone I literally just met thought I should be focused on just him. Why in the world would anyone do that? You don't even know the person. I can see why so many women are single who don't want to be. So you meet a man on a dating website, he asks you out, and now you can't follow-up with anyone else? I think not. Trust me: the men aren't talking, e-mailing, or texting only you.

Trust me: the men aren't talking, e-mailing, or texting only you.

I had another funny experience. A man asked if he could text me and then couldn't remember to whom he was replying. I called him on it, not because I was angry; I don't even know him. He should write things down and keep track, or he may end up alienating the woman he wants to pursue. And the same goes for us.

When I was growing up, my parents had time frames on how long we could talk on the phone with our friends or with boys. They also kept tabs on when people could call, where we could meet, and how long we could visit. What amazes me is how women who date today have no boundaries when it comes to men. Either they are so desperate for a man, or so afraid of making them angry, that they don't set limits. It really is OK to let a man know when he can call you—hence, your availability. You shouldn't be available 24/7 to a man who is not your husband. In fact, in the real world, even married women aren't available 24/7.

My late husband used to call me at work every day, sometimes a couple of times or more. He would catch me going to a meeting or in the middle of something, and I would say, "Honey, I can't talk to you right now. Is it an emergency? OK, we can talk when I get home." Of course, I felt loved, wanted, and valued by his attention, but I just couldn't talk—and he was my husband.

What gets me is that women who aren't even married will drop everything they are doing (including their kids) to pick up the phone because someone they are dating is calling. I know we get excited when a man we are interested in calls, but being available is one thing, being overly available is another. Most men respond well when they know a good time to call. They won't get voicemail, be interrupting your work, infringing on your time with your children, and they know they will have your full attention.

Now remember, I am talking about friendship and dating. It is OK to set good boundaries. It is not what you say but the way that you say it. Many women are jaded and hard and just deliver the message like a drill sergeant because they are so afraid of getting hurt or looking like a beck-and-call girl.

Once a man singles you out and asks you to be in an exclusive relationship with him, he is eliminating direct competition in the pre-courtship stage with you. Don't make assumptions about this transition. It is not bad to ask questions when a man says, "Can we be exclusive?" You should then ask questions like:

"What do you mean by exclusive?"
"How long would you like to do this?"
"Why do you want to do this?"

Remember, we are not eighteen years old. We are women in our thirties, forties, and up and are not playing games with our time and our lives. We don't have all the time in the world. These questions are reasonable and will prevent misunderstanding on both sides.

Remember the chapter "Silly Women"? We need to ask the right questions at the right time and not take anything for

granted. If the answers are not to your satisfaction, don't get angry, just stay friends. Now if the man you are friends with isn't mature enough to handle your decision, either way, he should be. Right? Move on, but whatever you do, don't let a man isolate you to himself

Don't be so desperate to be with someone that you lose your common sense.

without knowing why he wants to do it, period. Don't be so desperate to be with someone that you lose your common sense.

Courtship

Courtship is an old word that best describes the pure pre-engagement process. Courtship happens when a man makes it clear that he wants to consider marriage with you and you agree that you want to consider marriage with him. It doesn't mean you have received a proposal that has been accepted; otherwise, you would be engaged. This is the big opportunity you both have been waiting for. Courtship is a chance to go a little deeper and learn more about how each other thinks and what your values and goals are in life. This opportunity allows you to see if you can accomplish your dreams together.

I would hope you already have been honest with the man you are dating, but courtship is the time to ask the "why" behind the "what" questions. Dig deeper to understand the man's approach to problem solving and his coping mechanisms. Hopefully you will meet more of his friends and family and start building relationships with them. This is the does-she/he-fit-in-the-big-picture-of-my-life stage. As friends and even in exclusively dating, you can see the man with you personally, but what about the big picture of your life?

Take me for instance: I am a widow. I have adult children and grandchildren. I am a professional woman, a pastor involved in my church, and now an author. I have to consider if the man I am with can take this on. I also have to weigh whether or not I fit into his life. Men in my age bracket are established in their lives and careers and have their own accomplishments and things they are doing as well; therefore, we have to see if we

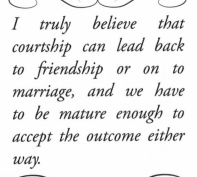

I truly believe that courtship can lead back to friendship or on to marriage, and we have to be mature enough to accept the outcome either way.

can bring our two lives together. A courtship provides an opportunity to see if we can or not. I truly believe that courtship can lead back to friendship or on to marriage, and we have to be mature enough to accept the outcome either way.

Again, I am not a proponent of long serial, monogamous relationships with older couples. It is ridiculous to think that two people over forty can't figure out if they can bring their lives together or not. As friends, you either developed a respect and admiration for each other's achievements and endeavors, or you just didn't mesh. Why move forward when you already know the man wants a woman who will focus only on him, his career, and activities, and you aren't giving yours up? Why ruin a good friendship with a failed courtship? When you are older, it is a given that both women and men are more set in their ways, and during the courtship phase, you must continually ask yourself, "Can I live with that if it never changes?"

I am telling you as a marriage veteran that what you saw in the beginning when you were falling in love rarely changes; it just matures. Now don't get me wrong, if things are flat out wrong and ungodly, most strong Christians will change those things because of their relationship with God, not because of their relationship with you. I am talking about changing habits, ways of thinking, approaches to life, and problem solving.

My late husband was always late; yes, all the time, from the day I met him until his death. He had a grace on his life for sure because this included being late to work, to church, and to our children's school events. Of course, he got better at being on time or even early (rarely), but his sense of timing never changed. I got used to it, worked around it, and stopped fighting it. I am very decisive and like to move quickly in decision-making; my late husband never fully embraced that, and guess what? It never changed either. We adjusted to each other, balanced each other out, and operated in our strengths.

If you see something during the courtship that you cannot live with, stay friends.

If you see something during the courtship that you cannot live with, stay friends. Some people want to try to make it work, but you don't *try* marriage. That mentality contributes today to the over 50 percent divorce rate. Sometimes we think we are so wonderful (this goes for men too) that we can mold and shape a person into what we want. Or we marry someone a lot younger than we are and think we can control

him/her. NO! A person will only change if he/she wants to. Any other motivation doesn't last.

The purpose of courtship is to see if you should be engaged and, shortly thereafter, get married.

Once courtship begins and you have an exclusive relationship with one man, that doesn't mean you start acting like an engaged or married couple. The purpose of court-

ship is to see if you should be engaged and, shortly thereafter, get married. I am a strong believer in having mentors in your life whom you can talk to about major life decisions. I do. I am an intelligent, independent woman, but I have a couple of "mom" figures, my own mother, and some married couples in my life who really know me. I can confide in them and talk to them about decisions.

If the people who know you aren't supportive, take a second look. A true mentor can actually tell you what to do and you will do it. That is accountability. Just talking to people about what you are doing is not accountability. In an area as significant in our lives as relationships, we need to develop true accountability and make sure that the man we are falling in love with has accountability partners and mentors as well.

I will end this section with a story. I have a couple of single friends, one male and one female, one widowed and the other divorced, both in their late forties, who were seeing each other. The relationship moved quickly from friendship to courtship. After a couple of months, the man was ready to propose, set a date, and get married. He was every single woman's dream, right? Wrong! The lady found out she wasn't ready to get married again. The man knew what he wanted, was leading and giving direction to the relationship, and pursuing and painting a picture of their future together. But she realized she wasn't quite ready to be with someone exclusively. She was an empty nester, used to making all of her own decisions, and in her mind, she thought maybe they didn't have enough in common. Were they both attractive? Yes. Were they both mature and sensible? Yes. They are still friends, and courtship moved back to friendship for them. This all happened in a matter of five months or so, not five years.

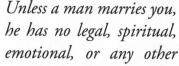

Marriage

I am not going to write a lot here. I will save it for my next book: *"A Game" Marriage is Work.* Let's just say that mar-

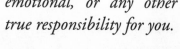

Unless a man marries you, he has no legal, spiritual, emotional, or any other true responsibility for you.

riage is commitment for men, period. Unless a man marries you, he has no legal, spiritual, emotional, or any other true responsibility for you. Marriage is a sacrificial covenant between a man and a woman, before God and witnesses, and binds you together spirit, soul, and body.

No other relationship compares to marriage: not the mother/child, brother/sister, or friendship-type relationships. You see more people devastated by divorce than by sibling rivalry. Marriage is an ultimate commitment that you make to another person, and when you break that commitment, you don't leave unscathed. That is why the traditional vows state, "Do not enter into this covenant unadvisedly" or without clear, concentrated thought and reflection.

I have lost one of my parents, a child, and my husband, and I can testify that the pain for each is very different. My husband and I were not related by blood, but we were bound to one another in a way I could never be with my father or my son. Spiritually, we two became one flesh. His death was a tearing away that requires healing on a different level.

I will finish with this: Once you are engaged, it only takes

Set a mutually agreeable date, and get married, or go back to being friends.

about three to four months to plan a great wedding; hence, don't become a forever fiancée and participate in an endless engagement. If you are not having sex, guess what? Your fiancée will want to marry you ASAP! I told my children that when I remarry, they won't see me for a whole month because I will need an extra long honeymoon.

Don't be satisfied with an engagement ring and no date set. Real commitment for men is marriage. If he is hesitating on setting a date, remember that you are older and should know what you both want. Ask him why he's hesitating. Get to the bottom of it. Set a mutually agreeable date, and get married, or go back to being friends.

Questions to Consider

1. What is your strategy for building healthy, true friendships with men?
2. What types of activities will you do with these men?
3. How will you prepare yourself for courtship (when asked)?
4. How will you prepare yourself for the two possible ends to courtship: marriage or going back to friendship?

THE ART OF
THE PURSUIT

(Hansel and Gretel and other Fairy Tales)

I have to admit that I had forgotten how strange some of the fairy tales were that I read when I was a child. *Hansel and Gretel* is downright scary, and it would make a great scary movie, right along with *Little Red Riding Hood* and *Snow White*. So why am I using it as an example? To make a point about the courtship process, of course. Sometimes men need a little help finding their way to you. Men want to please us, but they don't know how to go about doing so. It is very easy to lose patience because we wonder, "Why don't they get it?" or, "Why don't they do this or do that?" I am right there with you, but here is the reality: his not being able to find his way to you may continue after you are married, so learning this is very important, not just for a wonderful courtship but also for a happy marriage afterward.

I remember more times than I want to count, hearing my late husband saying to me, "Why don't you just tell me what you want or what you want me to do? It will be so much easier, and you won't be so frustrated." My first thought would be, *That takes all of the fun out of it. You don't want to have to figure it out.* Well, I was right. He didn't want to figure it out, and that never changed. I just accepted what he was saying and took that at face value. He was successful in pleasing me and happy, and I was no longer frustrated. See how that all miraculously worked out?

There will be no more disappointing birthdays, anniversaries, or Christmases when he has a clear understanding. Life is so much simpler than we make it: simple, but not easy.

If we are honest with ourselves, to some degree, we all buy into the fairy-tale romance and the happily ever after.

If we are honest with ourselves, to some degree, we all buy into the fairy-tale romance and the happily ever after. This does affect our expectations and approach to relationships with men. Add in the romantic chick flicks, romance novels, and the emphasis on Valentine's Day, and we are set up for disappointment in one way or another.

I still believe we can have the happily ever after because I am a romantic girl at heart, but the way we get there may not be like a fairy tale. I don't believe that chivalry is dead or heroes rescuing the lady in distress are non-existent, but chivalry and men's rescues are not rewarded in the real world the way they used to be. Many of today's women act as if they no longer need a door opened, an escort across a busy street, or a rescue of any kind. I know this is a broad generalization and that all women don't feel that way. However, when confronted with being unmarried and wanting to be, we get defensive and say things like, "I don't need a man to take care of me or my kids!"

or, "I can buy my own car; get my own house ..." Although we may, by necessity, be able and willing to care for ourselves, our children, elderly parents, and whoever needs our help, it doesn't mean we should.

I love the scripture in Genesis 2:18 that says, "It is not good for man to be alone, so I will create a helper for him." By deductive reasoning, we can say that it is not good for woman to be alone either. God said everything was good in His creation until man was alone. Then came woman. We are so special to God and to the man He created!

Now take a look at this very strange fairy tale, just an excerpt, so that you can get where I am going with this whole "pursuit" thing.

The two children had also not been able to sleep for hunger, and had heard what their step-mother had said to their father. Gretel wept bitter tears, and said to Hansel, "Now all is over with us."

"Be quiet, Gretel," said Hansel, "do not distress yourself, I will soon find a way to help us." And when the old folks had fallen asleep, he got up, put on his little coat, opened the door below, and crept outside.

The moon shone brightly, and the white pebbles which lay in front of the house glittered like real silver pennies. Hansel stooped and stuffed the little pocket of his coat with as many as he could get in. Then he went back and said to Gretel, "Be comforted, dear little sister, and sleep in peace, God will not forsake us," and he lay down again in his bed.

When day dawned, but before the sun had risen, the woman came and awoke the two children, saying, "Get up, you sluggards. We are going into the forest to fetch wood." She gave each a little piece of bread, and said, "There is something for your dinner, but do not eat it up before then, for you will get nothing else."

… When at last they awoke, it was already dark night. Gretel began to cry and said, "How are we to get out of the forest now?"

But Hansel comforted her and said, "Just wait a little, until the moon has risen, and then we will soon find the way." And when the full moon had risen, Hansel took his little sister by the hand, and followed the pebbles which shone like newly-coined silver pieces, and showed them the way. (www.mordent.com/folktales/grimms)

OK, if you can get over the mean, weird mom and dad dragging the children out into the forest and leaving them all alone, do you get it? The idea is that sometimes you need to drop a few pebbles or bread crumbs. Sometimes in order to get "out of the forest," we need to leave a path back home. Hansel and Gretel had to use bread crumbs the second time because the mean mom caught on. I know, very weird. What were our parents thinking, letting us read this as kids?

The next thing I usually hear is, "Tell me what the 'bread crumbs' are and how to leave them so I can get my man." Be patient, there are no pat answers here. That is why what we are talking about is called "the art of the pursuit."

It is important for every woman to have her own unique, pleasant fragrance, naturally and spiritually speaking.

To help clarify what I mean, let's talk a little about fragrance. I do a session in my single women's groups called "Perfume, Panties, and Prayer." What I will focus on here is the perfume part of that session. It is important for every woman to have her own unique, pleasant fragrance, naturally and spiritually speaking.

Sometimes Christian women think that you can separate the natural and the spiritual, but you cannot. We focus on the inner beauty and neglect the proper outside maintenance, and trust me, men don't overlook that. Men tend to be driven by their five senses more than we are, but even the Bible says that "... the Lord looks at the heart" (1 Samuel 16:7). We can strive to be more like Jesus, but just remember that He is the only one who can truly see the heart.

Excellence in character is not separate from excellence in appearance.

People's attention to detail and their actions are a reflection of what is going on inside their hearts. It is difficult to separate the two. Excellence in character is not separate from excellence in appearance. Work with what you have, and make your best presentation. As women, we must ask ourselves, "What kind of spiritual fragrance do we emanate? Is it sweet, attractive, exciting, and welcoming, or does it smell funny, is it hard to pick out, or does it stink?" If we want a man to pursue us, he must first be attracted to us both naturally and spiritually. You can have a beautiful, flawless outward appearance and yet give off a funny smell.

A woman who is fresh out of a failed relationship, who is insecure, competitive with other women, overly flamboyant, jealous, stuck-up, phony with others, hyper-spiritual, antagonistic, or hard can give off a strange fragrance that will keep the men she really wants away from her. Good men, who are looking for a wife not a "lay," do experience some fear, trepidation, and anticipation when they approach women;

therefore, if you are giving off weird vibes, either in your appearance or attitude, they may never approach you.

No one is responsible for our fragrance except us. Enjoying and embracing life, being happy with ourselves, pursuing our dreams, and making and keeping friends is our responsibility. It is easy to blame others, our past, parents, siblings, old boyfriends, ex-husbands, and friends who let us down. Ultimately, however, we control our attitudes, thoughts, and actions.

By the way, the practical, sensory side of fragrance is equally important. Do you have a perfume that smells fabulous on you? You should. Go to a department store, get several samples to take home, and try each one out for a week. See which one gets you the most compliments, and buy that one. Wear it every day, and especially when you go on that special date. Leave your natural and spiritual scent—your sweet-smelling aroma—behind in his car. It doesn't hurt to have a mini of your perfume to spray right before you leave his car, especially if he compliments you. It is a great idea for a lot of reasons. Just think about it; now there is a bread crumb for you!

Logistics of the Pursuit: Drop Those Bread Crumbs

When someone is in pursuit of you, where are they physically located? No, it is not a trick question. Think about it. That person is behind you. Women get it wrong. We think if a man is pursuing us then he should be in front, being strong, telling us what to do, and setting the pace. We ask ourselves the question, "Why isn't he doing this or doing that?" We expect him to be in front of us. The last time I checked, when you

The last time I checked, when you are being chased, the person is behind you.

are being chased, the person is behind you. It is no different in the game of love.

God did a great job balancing the process between men and women. A man you like is interested in you. How do you know? He calls, he asks you out, he watches you, he looks at you, and he finally makes a move, right? If you are not sure, what do you do?

Remember junior high and high school? This is where social media, texting, and communication technology falls short. They take personal, face-to-face contact off the table. Back in the day, you would ask one of your friends to ask one of his friends if he "liked" you or not, right? This would give you some assurance that dropping a bread crumb would be appropriate. In today's world of one-night stands and first-date hookups, your bread crumb could be interpreted as an invitation to spend the night. What is a girl with standards to do?

One solution I see is to have a personal calling card with your name and contact information. Make it pretty and even scented. Remember to appeal to the five senses, and leave him with something that will remind him of you. With today's technology, you can always block someone after the fact to keep him from calling or e-mailing you again if the first time doesn't work out so well. If you meet someone and do not know when you will see him again, give him your card. He will call or he won't; either way, the is-he-interested question will be answered.

Also, look for opportunities for your friends to set you up with people to and provide situations that are conducive to meeting and getting to know men. We should not be

When a man is pursuing you, he is waiting for clues and cues from you that he is doing the right thing.

afraid of these opportunities; they are far more natural than putting your picture and profile on a dating website or waiting for a man to appear out of nowhere at your door or thinking you will meet him at church. Don't get me wrong, dating websites have been very helpful for some people and are a great way to get your feet wet again if you have been off the dating scene for a while. I met my husband in the social hall at our college, not at church, even though we were both very strong Christians. When a man is pursuing you, he is waiting for clues and cues from you that he is doing the right thing. Drop those bread crumbs!

Logistics of the Pursuit: Courting Towards the Next Step

Where is the man when he is courting you or engaged to you? Answer: he is beside you. A man who has asked you to exclusively date him is walking along beside you, looking at you for signals as to how fast or slow to take this next step. Let him know when he is moving at the right pace. Encourage what you like;

Let him know when he is moving at the right pace. Encourage what you like; discourage what you don't like.

discourage what you don't like. It is important to recognize that if you want an exciting, long, "until death do you part" marriage, you need to learn the art of being pursued. Trust me: there will be times when you will need to get him in the pursuit mode again after you are married. If you did the friendship part of your relationship right, the courtship stage should be the shortest stage of the process.

Once you allow a man to single you out, meaning you stop dating other men and he has your time exclusively, he needs

If a man tells you he is not looking for a wife or he is not ready to get married or you are not his type, believe him!

to get to the point. A man looking for a wife will get to the point quickly. A man who wants to be in a relationship, have a girlfriend, or have a friend with benefits will not. If a man tells you he is not looking for a wife or he is not ready to get married or you are not his type, believe him! Don't try to change his mind. Don't waste one more minute of your life being his girlfriend. You can still date him, but move on emotionally, and keep dating other men. A man who is looking for a wonderful wife will find you.

I was having dinner with my daughter, and we were discussing how she and her husband met as a result of an assignment for the single women's class I was teaching. The assignment was simple: get an escort for a formal dinner event. You don't have to be more than friends or romantically involved. Just let him know to wear a suit, pick you up, be nice to you and your friends, and take you home. Also tell him there will be eight other beautiful, single women there besides you. My daughter, being the good student she is, asked an old childhood friend. That guy kept her waiting too long, so she asked another guy, who is now her husband.

The other man never got back to her, but when she announced her engagement two months later, he called her and said, "If I had come to that event with you, could that have been me?"

Her answer was, "We will never know, will we?"

We have to be willing to move on and not let the lack of a response on the part of men keep us waiting. God had the right man for my daughter. She loves him, and he loves her. He was looking for a wife and recognized one when he saw my daughter. I wish my late husband could have lived to see his only girl happily married and see her husband be the father of our beloved grandsons.

Logistics of the Pursuit: Marriage

Where is the man when he marries you? Where you have always wanted him to be: in front of you, leading you—at least, figuratively speaking. Ladies and gentlemen, keep this in the proper context. There may be women out there who just want a man to lead them. They want to stand quietly by, cleaning, cooking, having children, and meeting their husband's sexual and emotional needs. There is nothing wrong with that; in fact, it takes a lot of energy, determination, and strength to do those things. Nevertheless, there are women who also want to be partners with their husbands in additional ways. They want to plan their futures together and be a dynamic duo while still maintaining outside interests and careers.

There is no one-size-fits-all for marriage. Each couple is unique and has different complementary strengths. If you are a Christian, then you follow the Bible when it comes to marriage, and the practical ways those things play out can be different. One of the great benefits of marriage is the whole idea of the two becoming one. I especially enjoyed being able to operate in my areas of strength while my husband operated in his. We were opposites in many ways and were able to complement each other, so we made a great team together. My children are still adjusting to the changes they see in me since the death of their father. I can no longer operate only in my strengths, but I must let the pendulum return to the middle and live life with more balance.

Let's face it; if you are already wife material, you don't just want a ring, you want the wedding. Don't be fooled by a proposal with no date in mind, as if you are making progress toward your goal. When a man proposes, he should be ready and prepared to marry you right then and there, even if you ask for three to four months or so to plan a great wedding. Remember, we are not celebrities who live

Let's face it; if you are already wife material, you don't just want a ring, you want the wedding.

our lives in front of a fan base. Nor are we trying to stay on the cover of a magazine. We are living real lives, and we know that commitment for men means marriage. Marriage is the endgame of the pursuit, and a great marriage requires mastery of the pursuit.

A Practical, Romantic Lesson from the Fairy Tale *Beauty and the Beast.*

Marriage is the endgame of the pursuit, and a great marriage requires mastery of the pursuit.

The power of transforming love is found in a woman's ability to set boundaries, be consistent, keep her standards, and yet love unconditionally no matter how bad things look. In *Beauty and the Beast,* Belle didn't know about the Beast's previous life, success, or his good looks. She saw he was selfish, bitter, and had given up on life, but she was able to see beyond those negatives. She didn't feel sorry for him, make excuses for him, wallow in his pity party, or become like him. Instead, in spite of her own imprisonment, she remembered who she was and changed the environment by her mere presence.

The Beast began his pursuit to win her love and affection, and the pursuit literally became life and death for him. He began to draw on his inner resources when he couldn't depend on his looks and charm to win her over. He realized she could appreciate his looks and charms, but he had to draw upon his depth of character that went beyond his outward looks.

As a result of Belle's living up to her stalwart character, he realized he had within him the seeds of change and transformation. He acted on what was already within him, and in the end, he not only regained himself as a man, but he also regained his kingdom and his very life. What he gained most of all was a wonderful woman and a loving wife. His life went up because of the influence and love of a virtuous woman.

> He who finds a wife finds a good thing,
> And obtains favor from the LORD.
> —Proverbs 18:21–23

A man who has never had a wife has only had a measure of favor over his life. Men just don't know what they are missing when they choose to play house rather than have a home. I heard a very well-known pastor say, "God is always right; He is never wrong." That sounds redundant, but it is necessary to make the point. There is such an uplift that happens when a man finds the right wife—and it happens in both of their lives. That is why two are better than one. There is no substitute for favor, and favor only comes from God! Now that sounds like a fairy tale I can live with! How about you? See, I do have a sensitive, empathetic, loving side.

There is no substitute for favor, and favor only comes from God!

Questions to Consider

1. What two other ways can you think of to drop bread crumbs for a man who is interested in you?
2. How would you describe your spiritual or attitudinal fragrance?
3. What attitudes have you identified that need to change to adjust your fragrance?
4. Are you comfortable with the stages of the pursuit?

ESCORTS AND
HUSBAND PRIVILEGES

What is a lady to do if she is required to attend a formal event, an after-five cocktail party, a sorority gala, an auction/fundraiser, an opera, a concert, or an evening wedding? Should she get dressed in her finest dress, call a couple of girlfriends, and hit the road? Well, that is certainly a viable option, but who wants to do that? I certainly don't, at least, not on a regular basis. It is one thing to attend an event without an escort when you are married; it is a whole other feeling when you are a widow and attend the very same event. Something, or better yet, someone is definitely missing.

Now I know there are women out there who'd say, "What else is new? Get over it! Welcome to the world of being single!"

Well I say, "What a shame. Where are the gentlemen out there who know how to be friends and escort a lady to an event when needed?"

I ask myself, "Do I know any single men who would be willing to keep me company and escort me to a concert or wedding or special event should I need it?" The answer I get is, "Yes, there are." Do you want to know why? I thought you might. The main reason I believe so is because men like to be needed, and they don't mind being in the company of a well-put-together, attractive woman who is fun and easy to talk to. The fact of the matter is that he is more attractive to other women if he is seen with someone else, and so is the woman. The best part about the whole scenario is that it works out well for both people involved: they get to look their best, be comfortable, and have a great time together with no pressure.

In my world, and I hope in yours, men are very much needed, and it is not an act or a line to say so. If that were not the case, I would not be writing this book. There is absolutely nothing wrong with letting them know how very much they are needed. Yes, as single women, we have learned and can do many things on our own. I don't want to get used to that in my life. I miss my father, late husband, and late son tremendously for many reasons, and I don't intend to get self-sufficient permanently. Just because we can go to a special event alone doesn't mean we should. I may be a little old-fashioned in this area, but it was how I was raised: by a gentleman and a lady.

Before we go any further, let's look at the www.merriam-webster.com dictionary definition of the word *escort:*

> One that accompanies another for protection, guidance, or as a courtesy. Synonyms: attendant, companion, guard, and guide

I just love this definition. I need some protection, guidance, and to be treated with courtesy. Yes, I will take some of that. As you can see, *escort* does not mean to pay for a man to take you somewhere and then have sex with you later. It is also

I need some protection, guidance, and to be treated with courtesy.

important to understand that your escort shouldn't necessarily be someone you are interested in dating. He can be, but that is dangerous. I firmly believe that getting back to the idea of having an escort to an event is moving our thinking in a normal direction and re-engaging our abilities to relate to men on a number of levels: as friends, companions, potential dates, and potential husbands. One of the reasons online dating has taken off in the last ten years is because people are looking for a way to connect and meet. Who wants to show up at a social event alone or stag? Who wants to feel like an outsider because she doesn't have a boyfriend and, therefore, can't attend certain events without looking funny? Well, we don't.

I introduce this idea when I work with single women during my workshops. The final assignment for the women is to attend an event where an escort is required. This is very difficult for so many of the women because they usually only approach men they are interested in dating. They may have preconceived ideas about their male friends, or more often than not, they don't have any male friends. I will admit that you will run the risk of a man becoming interested in dating you once you have spent some time with him. However, if you are honest on the front end by stating your intentions for asking him to escort you, the responsibility falls squarely on his shoulders if he falls for you after the fact. If he does ask you out on a date later, go out with him. Why not?

Example One

The finale event planned for my very first group was a formal dinner banquet held by my local church. The dress required was suit and tie for men and semiformal to formal attire for the women. I set a few rules for the women. They had to wear a dress, at least three-inch heels, have their hair and make-up done, and get an escort who they were not interested in dating. I don't know why this is so difficult to understand. I also told the ladies to let him decide if he should drive or take them out after the banquet.

I reserved the tables and waited for the ladies to arrive. All but two showed up with an escort. They were relaxed, looked great, and had a reasonably good time. A few of us and the escorts went out to a local restaurant after the event to continue the evening. It was funny how that happened, and one of the gentlemen ended up paying for everyone.

In a debrief session later, many of the women said that going out with an escort wasn't as difficult as they thought it would be; and the men all said they enjoyed meeting so many attractive, fun women. Everyone had a great evening. As a result, two women in that group are now married (one married her escort), and one started dating her escort. Some of the women went back to their old ways that weren't working. Remember, it is your decision to change your thinking and actions.

It is your decision to change your thinking and actions.

Example Two

Another group of women participated in a finale event that included a little black dress, an Italian dinner, and ballroom dancing. Again, it was required they bring an escort. A huge discussion ensued about who would pay for dinner, who should drive, what if he didn't pay, and what was meant when

I said "little black dress"? Men are not that complicated and tend to rise to the occasion because they are naturally more competitive. I advised the women to be prepared to pay for dinner (although I knew they wouldn't have to), relax, and not grab for their purses as soon as the check came to the table.

I had a plan, of course, for the seating arrangement at dinner: the women sat across from their escorts, which forced them to make eye contact, smile, be nice, and talk with each man on either side. This should have been easy and natural if they didn't invite a man they secretly wanted to date. The men seemed to be enjoying all of the attention, and dinner went smoothly. When I was ready to order (yes, I had an escort, a family friend), my date immediately said to put my order on his bill. Guess what happened? Yes, you guessed right, the next man did exactly the same thing.

After dinner, we moved to another location for the ballroom dancing. That was an experience for me, as I learned to salsa for the first time. The group ranged in age from twenty-seven to seventy. As we continued dancing and switching partners, each and every man thanked me for having the event and expressed how much they had enjoyed the evening and meeting each and every lady. You think? Of course they enjoyed it. What hot-blooded American man wouldn't love the opportunity to spend the evening in the company of twelve single, attractive, dressed-up, happy women?

Speaking of that, an illustration of my book title occurred with this group. One of the gentlemen who came as an escort had a girlfriend. He came as an escort to an

What hot-blooded American man wouldn't love the opportunity to spend the evening in the company of twelve single, attractive, dressed up, happy women?

event where he knew twelve single women would be. He knew he would be having dinner and dancing with these twelve women. That is why, say it with me, "Girlfriends don't matter." Did he ask his girlfriend if he could go? He says he did. My point is this: being a man's girlfriend is not

My point is this: being a man's girlfriend is not as significant to him as it is to you.

as significant to him as it is to you. Maybe she was fine with it, maybe she wasn't. He came. I'm just saying.

At the writing of this book, I am planning the finale event—my exclusive book launch party—for any women who have attended my single women's groups or workshops. They cannot attend without an escort, they must RSVP, and be dressed in an after-five cocktail dress. They also must have their hair and make-up done. I will blog about how it all turns out!

Ladies, you do not have to attend formal or social events alone. Learn to ask for an escort without a motive, and see what good things will come from it. Mostly, you will boost your confidence and have more fun.

Now we are more confident, know how to ask for and get an escort to special events, and enjoy the company of a gentleman. One thing I know about men: even if they don't think they know what a gentleman is, they will do their absolute best to impress you if they value your opinion. They will rise to the occasion.

If a line gets drawn, the woman is the one who will have to draw it.

Where do we draw the line with the men we date and still get to the altar? That is the million-dollar question, right?

If a line gets drawn, the woman is the one who will have to draw it. Do you know any people who won't take something that is handed to them for free? They will take it, even if they think it is fake, because it cost them nothing. It is human nature to place a lesser value on something of low or no price.

You are valuable and do not have a low or non-existent price. You are a virtuous woman, and the Bible says that "her price is far above rubies," and "the heart of her husband safely trusts in her" (Proverbs 31:10–11). Now, welcome to the concept of husband privileges.

Husband Privileges™

Many women are consumed with the idea of doing whatever it takes to get and keep a man. They go so far as to become a "desperate wannabe housewife" (see chapter 7). I hope you didn't read chapter 7 first because it may have been hard to take without reading the first chapter. I wanted you to know where I was coming from. I am speaking to you from the perspective of a woman who married at nineteen years of age and stayed married for twenty-nine years, until "death do us part." My perspective is that there are things I have only done for my husband, and I consider them husband privileges. These privileges include a lot more than sex. I will restate here that all of the things in chapter 7 are husband privileges, and there are more.

I had a man tell me I was old-fashioned and out-of-date if I expected a man to take me out, buy me dinner, show me a good time over and over again,

It is insulting to think that my time, attention, company, pleasant conversation, affection, gentle touch, and even kiss are "nothing" to a man.

and then get nothing in return. Well, I know the "nothing" he meant was not having sex. It is insulting to think that my time, attention, company, pleasant conversation, affection, gentle touch, and even kiss are "nothing" to a man. I know better than that. My response to that statement, simply put, is this: I don't need a lot of men to get it about how I handle myself; I only need one. That man, more than likely, will become my new husband, and he won't ever have to look in the face of another man on this planet who will know me as intimately as he does. That includes spirit, soul, and body.

Ladies, how many men get the privilege of knowing your deepest desires, secret fears, crazy uncle, past mistakes, ex-husband or boyfriend details, spirituality, family drama, or body? I say only one: the man who marries you! We all have a desire to be known and intimately close to another human being in a romantic relationship. This desire drives us to give up so much more than we should to men who are undeserving of our devotion. We are just waiting for a title like "girlfriend" or "fiancée" as an excuse to start acting like wives when we are not wives.

How does a man know you care if you are not giving him your body, working at his business, sharing your money, helping him with his homework, or having his children? The same way the rest of the people in your life do: by your words, appropriate emotional

Marriage is a big step, and it requires a 100 percent commitment from both the man and woman, not 50/50, and it is too valuable to attempt to playact in advance.

support, and friendship. Marriage is a big step, and it requires a 100 percent commitment from both the man and woman, not 50/50, and it is too valuable to attempt to playact in advance.

Bottom line: marriage is a lot of work. Why wear yourself out playacting with man after man who will never marry you?

Husband privileges fall into three main categories: spirit, soul, and body. It should be seen as honor and respect by a man when his wife gives to him in these areas. Why are these privileges valuable to a man from his wife and not from his girlfriend? Simply because it is a big deal for a man to give a girl his name, access to his finances and reputation, and most importantly, his freedom. Now some men give some of these things to their girlfriends, but don't kid yourself, his freedom and name are intact and don't belong to you. Yes, I said it; someone had to! Who do you think came up with the terminology of "ball and chain," a man or a woman? Have you ever heard a woman say she is "tied down" with a husband?

There are too many examples of men who date women for long periods of time and never marry them. Then just a few years, or sometimes only a few months, after breaking up with the long-term girlfriend, they marry someone else. No one believes they actually did it, including all of the ex-girlfriends, and they set out on a mission to find out what this new wife did that they didn't do to get the ring. There is usually a good reason why a long-time, confirmed bachelor hasn't married: either he has some serious issues and is in denial, or he hasn't met a woman he wants to give up his freedom for. Men get to do the asking most of the time, and when they don't ask, there is a reason.

There are too many examples of men who date women for long periods of time and never marry them.

I have known some notorious ladies' men who many women thought would never marry, and then they did. Why? Because they met women who would settle for nothing less and would not treat them like husbands when they weren't husbands. When I was dating my husband, he would ask me to do things like his laundry or cook for him on a regular basis, and he wanted me to be available any time. I told him I knew how to do laundry and cook and that I would be happy to do those things for my husband when I got married. Now I did make a few of his favorite apple pies just to let him know I am quite a good cook, but do his laundry and be his beck-and-call girl? Nope!

I will never forget the time he wanted me to get up, get dressed, and come over to his dorm room at 11 P.M.—all the way across campus, in the snow. I asked him if it was an emergency. He said, "No." So I told him I would see him after class the next day. Are you serious?

A couple of years later, after we were married, I lost track of the times I had awakened in the middle of the night to pick him up from the team bus or airport, in the snow, when he would return home from a basketball road trip or mission trip overseas. I was happy to do so; after all, he was my husband, and having his wife there to meet him was and is a husband privilege.

I mentioned earlier in the chapter about husband privileges falling into three main categories: spirit, soul, and body. In a marriage, men need to be ministered to, or taken care of, by their wives in all three of these areas. If you do this as a girlfriend, wow, stop it!

Spiritual Husband Privileges—Prayer, Fasting, Intercessions

A man who honors a woman by making her his wife should receive from her spiritually in the areas of prayer, fasting, and intercessions. Giving to a man in this way definitely should be reserved for your husband. You can pray for a man you date or your male friends, but certainly not with them or with the dedication you should reserve for your husband.

I realize everyone reading this book may not be a person of faith, but I am. I know how much my late husband valued the fact that I would take time to listen to his needs and agree with him in prayer for his career, as well as for our marriage, children, finances, ministry, and life we were building together. I would do this for or with no other man, with my husband as my first priority. Individually, I pray for my children, grandchildren, family, and myself. But a husband's goals, needs, and desires are especially worth fasting and making intercession for. This same level of prayer and concern ought not to be the privilege of a boyfriend, significant other, wannabe husband, live-in lover, or companion.

> Confess your trespasses to one another, and pray for one another, that you may be healed. The effective, fervent prayer of a righteous man [woman] avails much.
>
> —James 5:16

The word *righteous* in the context of this verse means "right standing." As his wife, I can be in right standing in my husband's life and before God. I can kneel and pray and ask on behalf of my husband, knowing my prayers are being heard.

Pray for contentment, wisdom, and readiness to walk into your destiny when the right man finds you.

I realize as you move through the process of falling in love, you will pray for the man; I know I will. My point here is about the appropriateness of those prayers and their purpose. I have friends I pray for, but I stay on the right side of the emotional line because prayer will draw you to the one you pray for and create intimacy that only you may feel. Also, don't make the mistake of trying to pray a specific man into your life. That sets you up for disappointment. Pray for contentment, wisdom, and readiness to walk into your destiny when the right man finds you.

Soul Husband Privileges—Mind, Will, Emotions

The second main area of husband privileges has to do with your man's ego and his need to hear how much you respect and admire him. Many women get and keep a man's attention because they become master players of his emotions. Don't get me wrong, there is absolutely nothing wrong with letting a man know what you like about him, how well he did something, or how hot or good looking he is. The husband privilege is the responsibility you take in making sure he knows daily, all the time, how good he is. You will not be lying either, because you would not have married him if you didn't really admire him.

May I make a suggestion here? Please don't marry a man you don't truly admire and respect. Admiration and respect are hard to fake. A man will know and figure it out, and when he does, you will be history in his life.

When a boyfriend says, "Baby, you aren't supporting me, you're not there for me. Why didn't you come to my event?" he is asking for

Please don't marry a man you don't truly admire and respect. Admiration and respect are hard to fake.

husband privileges. If you decide to attend any of his activities on a regular basis, or even one time, he should be saying, "Thank you," not asking for more. If he wants you to be his regular cheerleading squad, then he needs to marry you. After marriage, it should be guaranteed that you'll be there, unless you are sick, right? And you'll be there, with bells on, looking fabulous!

It is not your job as a non-wife to take responsibility for your boyfriend's emotional well-being and support. Be encouraging, helpful, and positive, just as you would with any other friend, if he doesn't respect that, well, that looks like a red flag to me. Either that or he's a man who needs to recognize he wants a wife and not a girlfriend.

Read the following list:

- A soft place to lay his head
- Someone always in his corner
- Constant encouragement
- Help figuring out a solution
- Personal cheerleader
- A comfortable home
- Reassurance
- A recharge station
- A place where he can relax

These are all husband privileges. This list is what a man should get and expect from his wife. A single man is supposed to be doing without these things; otherwise, why would he marry?

When I was dating my late husband, I cheered him up after a few games if they lost or he didn't play well. I let him know he was still great (because he was), but I didn't do this after every game. I didn't feel, nor was I, responsible for his emotional well-being. I was supportive, but he was doing his thing to get ready for the next practice and game anyway. That point certainly was proven when he broke up with me. He kept his scholarship. None of our grades suffered; the relationship wasn't that serious.

When we married a couple of years into college, the emotional attachment obviously became a lot more serious for us both. Why? Because he was my husband, and we were both invested and committed to each other's success and emotional well-being. I felt the bad games more and the losses more, but I also had the place in his life to reassure him, encourage him, and of course, distract him.

Body Husband Privileges—Sex, Healthy Lifestyle

A third area of husband privileges, where a lot of men focus before and after marriage, is your body and a healthy lifestyle. Let's face it ladies, men are driven by their five senses, and what

they experience of us through their senses is what endears them to us. They like a confident, attractive woman and someone they can have fun with. OK, I think we all get it, but don't take how much we are willing to cater to a man who is not our husband to

Being your husband's fantasy woman is a husband privilege.

the extreme. Did you read the chapter entitled "You are Not a Celebrity"? I hope so. It is not our job to become some fantasy woman for a man. If he wants a fantasy woman, I say go find one, and be with her; it's not me. I know my strengths and weaknesses and what I am good at; that is, what I have to offer. Being your husband's fantasy woman is a husband privilege. Who says there aren't some things that should be reserved for marriage?

Some women whom I love and respect very much tell me I would be a fool to not "try before I buy" in the area of his body and sex. There is no empirical evidence that trying before you buy makes for better marriages. Use your common sense. Look at the divorce rate. It doesn't matter if couples live together first, try out each other first, have children, don't have children, share money or not, buy a house first or after: couples are still getting divorced at the same rate. Sexual tryouts are no guarantee of a sexual satisfaction in marriage. I don't need a survey to know the truth of that statement. Besides all of those reasons, sexual satisfaction from your body is a husband privilege. Ask any happily married, sexually satisfied couple: they know how to keep it exciting and satisfying.

My faith is the primary driver for my position on this issue, but so are my common sense and personal standards of conduct. Some women believe, "If you've got it flaunt it," and there are plenty of takers. Choose to err on the side of discretion. When my children approached the dating age, I let them know I wasn't interested in seeing the parade. This especially applied to my sons. I specifically told them I didn't have the emotional time or energy to meet random women who would float through their lives before they decided on the one they wanted to marry.

As a result, I didn't meet many women or girlfriends. I met a couple of each son's girlfriends, neither of which they married. I met my older son's fiancée before he passed away, and I met and my youngest son's wife about one month before they were married. While I didn't intend it at the time, by accident, I was teaching my sons that there is a distinct difference between a girlfriend and a wife. They must have known the difference because there were quite a few I never met.

In today's society, men will introduce you to their children, family, ex-wives, and just about anyone else, so introductions are no indication of how they see you anymore. I imagine there are a few old-fashioned men out there who respect their parents in such a way that they would never bring a random girlfriend to meet them, but they are few and far between.

Keeping a man happy and being his favorite playmate is a husband privilege. When you have a satisfying friendship, then courtship with a man, he will ask you for more. All I am

Keeping a man happy and being his favorite playmate is a husband privilege.

saying is your response should be similar to the following: "I am looking forward to doing that with my husband, or for my husband." Guess what? If a man you are dating, wants all of the things I have discussed here and in "Desperate Wannabe Housewives," guess what he will do? You got it, become your husband! Of course, you run the risk that there is a silly woman next door or down the street who will give every privilege away for free. OK, so be it, but you are not the one who will.

Looking your best, being your best, and living a healthy lifestyle is a gift we give ourselves when we are single and to our husbands when we are married. His preferences become very significant in this area and should be listened to. A man who wants to dictate your life, tell you how often to work out, how to wear your hair, and what to eat and is not your husband has no right to do so. It is good to know how he feels. Make a mental note because it probably won't change over time. You will have to decide if you can you live with that kind of behavior,

Don't give a boyfriend something only a husband has earned.

because if you cannot, move on. You won't change him, even if he does marry you.

I firmly believe there is an amazing man out there who will be honored to buy you a beautiful engagement ring, marry you very quickly, put the wedding band next to that engagement ring, and gladly receive all of the husband privileges from you! You know why he will? Because of the high value he sees in you because you have valued yourself first! When a man gives up his freedom, gives you his name, allows you access to his finances, and supplies you with his protection and care, he becomes a husband and deserves to be treated like one. Don't give a boyfriend something only a husband has earned.

Questions to Consider

1. Evaluate your current/past non-marriage relationship(s). Are you treating or did you treat those men like a husband? What are you doing or did you do specifically?
2. List specific things from this chapter that are husband privileges.
3. How do you feel emotionally after reading this chapter?
4. Do you agree with the idea of "Husband Privileges™"? Why or why not?
5. What is the difference between the father of your children and the man who is your husband, if he is not both?

Last year, I was at Barnes and Noble bookstore, looking for a hard copy of a relationship book. I went to the music/DVD section of the store because the line was shorter. The young man behind the counter asked, "Can I help you?" I told him the book I was looking for, and he found it on the computer. Then he asked me if I believed the guarantee of the book that said if you weren't satisfactorily dating in six months, you could have your money back.

I told him, "Yes." Of course, this started a conversation about the whole concept of finding the right person in our lives.

I shared a little of my story about being a widow and being "out there" for the first time in thirty-four years. I asked him if he had a girlfriend, and he said he did. So I asked permission to ask a few questions for antidotal research for my book and my class for single women. He was all smiles and agreed. By the way, he was a very handsome man.

I asked, "How long have you been together?"

He answered, "Five years!"

"Wow! How is it going, and what are your intentions?"

"We're living together and have bought a condo together."

"You have been with her for five years, and you don't know if you want to marry her?"

"I'm not going to marry her!"

"Does she know this little bit of information? Do you ever want to get married?"

All I can say is wow! I told him he might want to tell her he is not going to marry her. Playing house doesn't mean you will ever have a home. Do I need to say it here? "Girlfriends don't …" You finish it.

12

FINAL THOUGHTS

This hurts me more than it hurts you. Well, I didn't either when my parents would say it to me, but disbelief didn't stop me from using the same rationale with my own children. It was worth a try, though. Breaking down mindsets, wrong thinking, and imaginations is very hard work. Sometimes when I thought it would only take a hoe (the kind you use to till the soil in a garden) to break up the soil, it felt like taking a jackhammer to concrete. When ideas are so deeply entrenched in our minds and the rut is so deep, sometimes the only solution is to create a deeper trench. This new,

When ideas are so deeply entrenched in our minds and the rut is so deep, sometimes the only solution is to create a deeper trench.

145

deeper trench hopefully becomes the default for where we go while under stress, and hopefully, it is the one of practiced good habits in our relationships.

It's Not Easy

It is not an easy undertaking to look at and evaluate our approach to relationships with men. Change can be terrifying and exciting at the same time. The bad news is that we may need a huge shift in our thinking process. The good news is that we will be taking the first step toward a healthy place in relating to men. Please recognize, I am not trying to turn you into every man's best friend. Who wants to be that and not be married? Who wants to be the woman men always come to for help on how to approach another woman or, worse yet, one of her own friends? We just must move away from the idea of putting all of our eggs in one proverbial basket by dealing with one man at a time.

Taking a positive view of men and relating to them is much easier when we are doing it from the context of having value-producing standards for our own personal behavior. I will repeat it again here: if we do not value ourselves and understand that we have something wonderful to offer, no one else will value us either. I am thankful for having a good sense of confidence and esteem instilled in me by my parents. More important is the identity I formed when I became a Christian at fourteen years old.

You may be wondering how I maintain a positive outlook on life. The scriptures and thoughts I will leave you with in this final chapter will hopefully answer that question and encourage you to join me in the journey forward.

This scripture from the Bible is an illustration of how important our thoughts are to living life in a healthy manner, and the approach is not one masses of people will take. I begin with

2 Corinthians 10:4–5 in three different translations to be sure the meaning is conveyed if you are not familiar with the Bible.

> For the weapons of our warfare are not carnal but mighty in God for pulling down strongholds, casting down arguments and every high thing that exalts itself against the knowledge of God, bringing every thought into captivity to the obedience of Christ …

> The world is unprincipled. It's dog-eat-dog out there! The world doesn't fight fair. But we don't live or fight our battles that way—never have and never will. The tools of our trade aren't for marketing or manipulation, but they are for demolishing that entire massively corrupt culture. We use our powerful God-tools for smashing warped philosophies, tearing down barriers erected against the truth of God, fitting every loose thought and emotion and impulse into the structure of life shaped by Christ. Our tools are ready at hand for clearing the ground of every obstruction and building lives of obedience into maturity. (MSG)

> We use God's mighty weapons, not worldly weapons, to knock down the strongholds of human reasoning and to destroy false arguments. We destroy every proud obstacle that keeps people from knowing God. We capture their rebellious thoughts and teach them to obey Christ. (NLT)

I love this! These verses mean we are to take every thought that is contrary to what we know is right and value-producing in our lives and relationships and conquer it! At points, I was pretty tough and hard core, and I won't apologize for that, but I do understand it can be painful to face a pattern of wrong thinking. The good news is that you can think differently. Get a couple of your best friends, and take this journey together. It is very important to take command of your thoughts. Your thinking guides your attitudes and actions, and we must work towards exercising deliberate control over our thoughts.

> Who shall separate us from the love of Christ? Shall tribulation, or distress, or persecution, or famine, or nakedness, or peril, or sword? ... Yet in all these things we are more than conquerors through Him who loved us. For I am persuaded that neither death nor life, nor angels nor principalities nor powers, nor things present nor things to come, nor height nor depth, nor any other created thing, shall be able to separate us from the love of God which is in Christ Jesus our Lord.
>
> —Romans 8:35, 37–39

We are all human, and we make mistakes. Additionally, some things happen to us in life that we did not count on nor bring on ourselves. The Bible recognizes this as fact, and yet it gives us hope that we can overcome, even in the worst of circumstances. I agree with you that the end of a relationship, be it a non-marriage or a marriage, causes trauma and distress and can be life-changing in a negative way. This is where our attitude in the circumstances either elevates us or levels us to the ground. The choice we make at that time and place matters. A delicate balance exists between living in the moment and having a plan for the future. We must do both, because life is long, and life is short.

A delicate balance exists between living in the moment and having a plan for the future.

We must make decisions considering long-term consequences, and at the same time, we must recognize when we need to do something right now. You may meet, or already know, the man who you will marry, and it may not take two years for you to come to that conclusion, like you had planned in your mind. You may just know. At the same time, you may have to pause and talk to a mentor, pastor, or friend before moving forward and end up tying the knot in a matter of months rather than years.

It has been very helpful for me to get grief counseling during the last couple of years. I am glad I have someone objective to talk to about the feelings that emerge, like anger, fear, an excitement to move forward while feeling bad, a desire to plan but being scared, and many more. All of these feelings can be confusing. Jesus knows we all need someone, sometimes many someones, to walk alongside us on this journey called "life." You may have had similar feelings arise as you read this book. Perhaps you recognized unresolved issues with past relationships or family, or you felt anger at yourself for poor choices. Here's the good news! You don't have to stay where you are. Move forward. Seek counsel. Be refreshed and renewed in your mind and spirit.

The movement from being a girlfriend to a wife happens before you start dating any man seriously. During this process, it is important to keep "girlfriend" status in its proper place in your thinking. If your desire is to be a wife, reserve some things for the man who marries you. Understand the pursuit and your role in it, and be willing to develop friend-

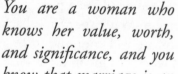

You are a woman who knows her value, worth, and significance, and you know that marriage is an enhancer of that value, not a creator of it.

ships with more than one man at a time. You are a woman who knows her value, worth, and significance, and you know that marriage is an enhancer of that value, not a creator of it.

There is now no condemnation for those who are in Christ
Jesus, who do not walk according to the flesh, but according
to the spirit.

—Romans 8:1

You are free to start over with a clean slate in your thinking.
Break up the fallow ground, and prepare your soil for a fresh,
life-giving relationship with a man. In my very first blog post
to promote this book, posted December 6, 2011, I stated one
of my goals for the book was to help women understand that
men don't consider the role and title of "girlfriend" as significant as women do. I hope you understand now, in light of the
privileges a marriage relationship contains and the high value
we place on those privileges and ourselves, that becoming a
wife is the result.

Most of the things I mentioned in this book are not new.
"That which has been is what will be, That which is done is
what will be done, and there is nothing new under the sun"
(Ecclesiastes 1:9). It is my hope that I have brought to the
surface and confirmed some underlying beliefs and have introduced some new ideas about dating, men, and relationships.

I didn't have a perfect childhood, and I haven't had a life
free from unexpected setbacks and tragedy. The one constant
for me will continue to be my faith in Jesus, and this faith
strengthens me in my resolve to run on and see what the end
will be.

Help me start a Relationship Revolution™! Imagine it
with me: confident, value-filled women of all shapes and sizes
who are open to building positive friendships with men. We
can eliminate some of the pain of breakups in non-marriage
relationships, have more stable lives, and help create an environment in which men can be men. We are successful and
competent but still very much appreciate a door opened, a chair
pulled out, and courteous treatment. We recognize men have

egos, and that can be a good thing. We will reserve Husband Privileges™ for our future husbands, will not try to practice being married while dating, and will not become desperate wannabe housewives. We understand that from a practical "what do I call you?" standpoint, we may be referred to as a girlfriend, even though it is not the long-term status we are seeking.

I encourage you to surround yourself with people who are positive, supportive, and generous with giving wise counsel. Literally begin the process of changing your mind. It is a woman's prerogative to change her mind, and this will certainly be a change for the better. I wish you the best in life and in love. Let's do it!

Questions to Consider:

1. In what ways were you challenged in your thinking regarding relationships with men?
2. What is the difference between a "girlfriend mentality" and that of a wife?
3. How do you plan to move forward?

ABOUT THE AUTHOR

Cheryl is a self-described military brat, the daughter of a three-War Veteran US Army Sergeant Major, and her mother, Juanita. She is the second oldest of five children and was born in Fort Dix, New Jersey. She has lived in Germany, Oklahoma, California, Indiana, and Washington State. She graduated from Lakes High School in Tacoma, WA, and Washington State University in Pullman, WA, with a B.A. in Business and an a M.B.A. Cheryl married Aaron Lee Haskins Sr. at nineteen years old, while in college. She has two living adult children, a daughter and a son, and four grandchildren. Her husband died in 2009, and her son Aaron Jr. died in 2011.

Cheryl worked in banking, taught high school and at private college, served as director of operations for a non-profit, owned her own custom sewing business for eight years, and is currently the executive director of a private foster care agency and preschool/kindergarten.

She is an avid quilter and belongs to Pacific Northwest African American Quilters and is also a member of Delta Sigma Theta Sorority. Cheryl was a candidate for public office in Renton, WA, in 2007 and counts it as a significant experience in her life.

Cheryl's faith in God is central to her life and has been since she became a Christian at fourteen years old. She served with her late husband on the pastoral staff of a local church in the Seattle area for eighteen years and continues on. She credits her sanity and resilience in the face of adversity to Jesus alone.

She resides in Washington State and plans to write more books in the future. For more information, visit Cheryl at:

- www.girlfriendsdontmatter.com
- Twitter: twitter@GFSdontMatter
- Facebook: Girlfriends Don't Matter
- Cheryl@girlfriendsdontmatter.com.

WinePressPublishing
Great Books, Defined.

To order additional copies of this book call:
1-877-421-READ (7323)
or please visit our website at
www.WinePressbooks.com

If you enjoyed this quality custom-published book,
drop by our website for more books and information.

www.winepresspublishing.com
"Your partner in custom publishing."